Sensational Silk

a handbook for sewing silk and silk-like fabrics

by Gail Brown

designed by Linda Wisner
illustrated by Priscilla F. Lee
Kathy Kifer Howell
Alison McKinley
Linda Wisner

Thanks to all the Palmer/Pletsch people — Marta Alto, Karen Dillon, Judy Lindahl, Pati Palmer, Susan Pletsch, Lynn Raasch, Roslyn Simon, Marilyn Thelen, Barbara Weiland and Leslie Wood.

Special thanks also to Ardis Koester, Ph.D., Extension Textiles and Clothing Specialist, Oregon State University; Bill Brandt, American Silk Mills; Ken Noonan, Schwarzchild Textiles; Pat McElhenny, Risdon Corporation, Sewing Notions Division; Cynthia Nugent, Rodolph (U.S. agents for Jim Thompson Silks of Thailand); Ann Lyng, Proctor and Gamble; Mala Biggs, Whirlpool Corporation; Dr. Dorothy Siegert Lyle, (International Fabricare Institute); Mildred Gallik, Soap and Detergent Association; Janet Klaer, Coats & Clark, Inc.; E.I. DuPont Nemours & Company, Inc.; Elna®, Kenmore® (Sears), New Home®, Pfaff®, The Singer® Company, Swiss-Bernina® and Viking® sewing machine companies; Armo Division of Crown Textiles; Pellon Corporation; Stacy Fabrics Corporation; Butterick Fashion Marketing Co. (Butterick and Vogue Patterns); Folkwear Pattern Company; McCall Pattern Company; Simplicity Pattern Company; International Silk Association; all the retailers, consumers and resources that generously offered valuable information for this book; and to Bobbie Keeney, my most proficient and patient typist.

Copyright ©Palmer/Pletsch Incorporated 1982. Eighth Printing 1989
Library of Congress Catalog No. 82-80827
Published by Palmer/Pletsch Associates,
P.O. Box 12046
Portland, Oregon, U.S.A. 97212-0046

Design and Production by Wisner Associates, Portland, Oregon
Illustrations by Wisner Associates
Divider page fashion art by Priscilla F. Lee
Printed by The Irwin-Hodson Company, Portland, Oregon

ISBN 0-935278-07-9

2

Home economist Gail Brown is a nationally known sewing expert, columnist and author.

After graduation from the University of Washington, she took her Clothing and Textiles degree to New York City and landed a job as a promotional consultant and, later, Marketing Director for one of the largest fabric companies. Since, she has been Communications Director for Stretch and Sew, Inc.

Her other titles include **Sew A Beautiful Wedding** (Palmer/Pletsch), **Super Sweater Idea Book** (Butterick/New Century Publishing), and **Instant Interiors**, a series of home decorating how-to booklets. Well-known for her thorough product and technique research, she is an active free-lance writer whose work has been featured in publications like *Handmade, Needlecraft for Today, Needlecraft News, Needle and Thread, Textile Booklist,* and *It's Me!* She is frequently called upon to demonstrate techniques from her books and articles for network and cable television appearances.

Gail is also a partner in Brown/Wisner, an Eugene, Oregon-based creative service agency specializing in sewing-related projects.

The busy writer lives on a 200 acre farm in rural Cottage Grove, Oregon with her husband, Steve Simpson, young daughter Bett, peacocks, wild ducks, Morgan horses, cattle, a dog and a cat. She very seldom gets everything done, but has fun trying.

TABLE OF CONTENTS

TABLE OF CONTENTS

CHAPTER ONE
Introduction

Silk. There's not another fiber so luxurious and perhaps so misunderstood. Throughout the 4,000 years of sericulture, silk, the work of a mere worm wonder, has been synonomous with high fashion, status and wealth. But because it fills this coveted niche in the textile world, many regard silk as too fragile and spendy for everyday wear.

Not so. Although certainly one of nature's finest fiber creations, silk is just that — natural — highly absorbent so it's comfortable in both warm and cold weather . . . possessing unparalleled strength for long-term durability . . . unusually resilient, minimizing bagging and sagging . . . plus, of course, it has that gorgeous luster and drape. And contrary to common belief, YOU CAN WASH MOST SILKS. I'll show you how easy and sensible it is in Chapter 3.

With the help of this book you'll too discover how simple sewing with silk can be. The techniques aren't difficult, just different. Remember, we're part of a generation that previously hasn't worn or sewn with silk. That's changing daily. A wider selection of more beautiful and affordable silks than ever before is now available in fabric stores.

Let's not forget those deceiving silk look-alikes either. Many will fool even the most discerning eye. The sewing is generally the same as for silks, but the "silkies" are less expensive, relatively care-free and more widely distributed in most areas.

No matter what your figure type, lifestyle, or sewing expertise, you'll love working with and wearing silks and silkies. You'll look and feel simply sensational.

CHAPTER TWO
How the Silks and Silkies Are Made

Legend tells us that silk was "discovered" 4,000 years ago when a cocoon dropped from a mulberry tree into the tea of a Chinese princess. As it softened she found it was possible to reel off a very strong, durable fiber from the cocoon . . . silk!

It's incredible to compare silk's ancient and colorful history to the relatively short life of today's synthetics, created, for the most part, to imitate silk.

1910 — Rayon — first called "artificial silk"

1924 — Acetate — developed to be even silkier than rayon

1938 — Nylon — introduced to be strong and silky

1953 — Polyester — created to have excellent strength and the versatility to imitate any natural fiber, including silk.

1968 — Qiana® — a type of nylon DuPont created to imitate silk while being more comfortable to wear than other synthetic fibers.

Now, man-made fibers account for nearly 75% of all the fibers used by American textile mills. Just a few years ago, real silk fiber made up only 1% of this production! But as the Orient opens up for mutual trade and the public's taste for real silk re-awakens, the use of the silk fiber and imported fabrics increases annually. Many mills and consumers have decided that the blending of silk fibers with synthetics and natural fibers results in the "best of both worlds" — comfort and luxury that's easy-care and affordable.

The Silk Making Process — One of Nature's Most Imitated Creations

The basic method of making almost all man-made fibers is a direct imitation of the silk worm miracle. Just as the silkworm extrudes liquid silk (a protein product) through a gland in its head, synthetics are made by forcing a chemical liquid through fine holes in a "spinneret" to form filaments.

The Cultivated Silk Story
courtesy of the International Silk Association

1. The silk moth lays eggs.

2. The moth larvae hatches.

3. First – fourth stage of larvae —

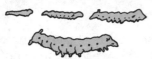

eating mulberry leaves. One acre of mulberry trees can provide enough leaves to raise 160,000 silk worms — who in turn produce enough silk fiber for 1300 square yards of fabric!

4. The fifth stage — matured larvae (pupa). NOTE: Stages 1-5 can happen in 28 days!

5. Cocoon-making in straw or cardboard nets (in about three days.) One worm can produce from 1000-4000 feet of silk fiber (123 cocoons for 1 square yard of crepe de chine). Since emergence of moth ruptures the cocoon filament the "pupa" is killed by steam or hot air.

6. Inside of regular and dupion silk cocoons.

7. Selection of cocoons.

8. Spinning out of each cocoon onto bobbins at silk reeling mill (filature) — or at home factory. Filaments from 5-10 cocoons must be used to form one silk fiber.

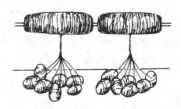

9. Making of silk yarn. Filaments from 2-4 bobbins are used to form one yarn. The yarn is twisted for strength.

10. De-gumming the silk.

Silk Terminology

Terms Relating to Silk and Silk Processing

Sericin — the natural silk "gum" that protects the fiber. It is usually not removed until after weaving. When sericin is removed, the fabric becomes much softer, lustrous and wearable (sericin can cause an allergic reaction).

Raw Silk — any silk yarn or fabric prior to the removal of the sericin. Seldom used in this form.

Weighted Silk — when metallic salts have been added to give the fabric extra body. Weighting comes out with washing or dry cleaning. Inferior silks can be weighted to appear higher quality (uncommon today).

Pure Silk — unweighted silk. Often this will be printed directly on the fabric.

Terms Relating To Fiber Length and Type

Spun Silk — short fibers, caused by tangling or when a cocoon is pierced by the emerging moth and broken into shorter lengths. The fibers are twisted together into a yarn that has less luster and strength than yarn made from long filaments.

Noil Silk — short waste fibers from the inner part of the silk cocoon. They are gathered up and spun into a yarn and then woven or knitted into nubby looking fabric with a dull surface. Frequently but inaccurately referred to as raw silk.

Dupion or douppioni — that is made when two silk cocoons join together. The fiber is uneven, irregular and large in diameter in places (slubbed). Used in pongee, shantung and other fabrics with an irregular slub texture.

Wild silk or tussah — fibers from the wild silk worm whose diet and environment haven't been controlled. Tussah is strong, but coarse and uneven, and produces a fabric with these same characteristics. It's generally used in its natural shade, but can be dyed in brilliant colors. Often wild silk fabric is also incorrectly called raw silk.

The Silky Synthetics Story

Rayon is made of regenerated cellulose, (cotton, wood pulp, etc.). Its care and wearing qualities are like other natural fibers.

The other silky synthetic fibers — acetate, nylon, triacetate and polyester — have different care and wearing qualities. They are called thermoplastic because they can be permanently shaped or creased with high heat (ever try to remove a hemline crease from perma-pressed pants?) And, they can melt with high heat (hence, permanent shine by over-pressing).

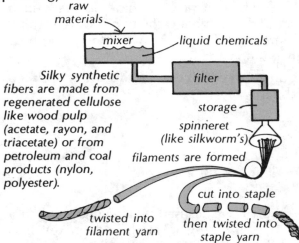

raw materials

mixer

liquid chemicals

filter

Silky synthetic fibers are made from regenerated cellulose like wood pulp (acetate, rayon, and triacetate) or from petroleum and coal products (nylon, polyester).

storage

spinneret (like silkworm's)

filaments are formed

twisted into filament yarn

cut into staple

then twisted into staple yarn

Holes can be a wide variety of sizes and shapes, effecting fiber and fabric characteristics. Silky yarns can be "textured" or reprocessed to alter the fabric characteristics adding stretch-ability, softer hand, pebbly or crepey surface, or resiliency.

Fabrics and Your Comfort

Is the fabric "comfort level" important? The more absorbent fibers are, the more comfortable they are to wear. They absorb body moisture and air humidity, so are less prone to static electricity and can be cleaned more easily. However, they often wrinkle more.

The less absorbent fibers are less comfortable, but wrinkle less, have better shape retention and can be more durable. Decide which qualities are most important to you and buy accordingly.

Silks and Silkies Absorbency Scale

Most absorbent Silk

Rayon

Acetate/Triacetate

Nylon (Qiana®)

Least absorbent Polyester

Finishing and yarn texturizing may alter this scale.

12

Fiber Length Determines Look of Finished Fabric

Silk is the only natural fiber that is naturally long. Both silk and synthetics can be cut into shorter lengths. Characteristics of the fabric can be changed by length of the fiber used in the following ways:

Filament Fiber — very long. Silk is the only natural fiber that is long naturally. Used in yarns that make fabrics smooth, with a high luster. They are strong, resilient and therefore wrinkle less.

Staple Fiber — short fibers that are twisted into a yarn that has a fuzzier surface. (Short silk fibers are called 'spun'.) Fabrics have less sheen and can have the appearance of cotton or wool. They can pill more due to the short ends (especially synthetics).

How Will Your Fabric Perform?

Quality is as varied as types of silk and silk fabrics. Especially when it comes to sewing, wearing and caring for these fabrics, the old adage "you get what you pay for" seems truer than ever. Don't waste your time on fabric that won't perform as you expected (see chart pg. 16).

• Does it wrinkle? Squeeze the fabric in your hand . . . silks will wrinkle more than silky synthetics, but do you care? I call them status wrinkles. I've found that wrinkles often "hang out" of quality silks in a few hours and prints can camouflage wrinkles. "Springy" synthetic fabrics can be wrinkle-free, but the extra resilience can mean less drapability.

13

• Is the fabric printed "on grain"? If not it will be difficult to cut out and possibly will not hang properly.

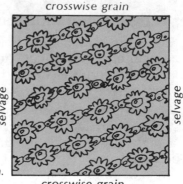

crosswise grain

selvage

selvage

Fabric printed off-grain.

crosswise grain

• Is the fabric dimensionally stable? Try pulling the fibers apart on the lengthwise and crosswise grains. Do the fibers separate easily? Most fabrics will separate slightly, but easy separation can indicate a loosely woven or unstable fabric (best for loose fitting styles that get less stress).

• Will the fabric hold its shape? Try the "thumb test" from **Mother Pletsch's Painless Sewing** book . . . pull a small section of the fabric with your thumbs and hold for five seconds. If it recovers quickly from the warmth and stress of your thumbs it will hold its shape in wear.

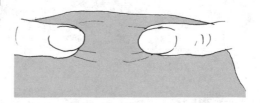

• How easily will the fabric be to sew? Ravelly and sheer fabrics necessitate seam finishing and special handling. Lighter and more slippery fabrics require more special sewing techniques. Knits are wonderfully forgiving, easy to sew, fit and wear . . . the silk and silk blend knits are sensational!

• Will the fabric be durable enough for the intended use? You needn't worry about a seldom-worn evening blouse — go ahead and choose a fragile lamé. But for a wardrobe basic? Consider quality crepe de chines, interlocks, surahs, shirting silks or poplins. Our durability scale on the following page should help you decide.

14

Weave Types and Durability*

 Leno Weave — an open weave made by twisting or twining the lengthwise threads in a continuous figure eight.

 Satin Weave — characterized by its beautiful shine. The surface is composed of "floats" or warp yarns which pass over several filling yarns. Because of "floating" yarns, satin fabrics snag more easily.

 Jacquard Weave — an intricate method of weaving used for complicated design patterns. Often reversible, with a combination of satin and plain weaves creating the motifs.

 Dobby Weave — made by a multiharness loom to form small, geometric figures. Expensive.

 Plain Weave — the most common weave. Each yarn in both the warp and filling run alternately over and under one another. Strength depends on the type of yarn and how tightly woven.

 Rib Weave — in this variation of the plain weave the yarns in one direction are heavier than in the other direction, creating the rib effect. Generally quite a durable fabric weave.

 Twill Weave — has characteristic diagonal lines that are more or less pronounced depending on the yarn weight and construction. Fabrics of this weave are strong, resilient, and often soil-resistant due to the yarn density. Because of the more complicated process, however, they can be more expensive than other weaves.

 Herringbone twill variation — the diagonal ribs switch back and forth in direction, creating the herringbones. Very durable.

*Durability may be altered by fiber and/or weave quality.

Least Durable ↑ **DURABILITY SCALE** ↓ **Most Durable**

Silks and Silkies — Fiber Characteristics and Care

Generic Fibers Brand Names/Trademarks	Characteristics	Care	Basic Burn Test Results*
Silk no "brand" names but see pg. 18 for companies and distributors.	Absorbent, comfortable, cool in summer, warm in winter Dyed colors and luster are unsurpassed Unusually fine "hand" and drapability Fair to good wrinkle resistance Can build up static electricity Weakened by direct sunlight, perspiration, anti-perspirants and chlorine bleach Resistant to mildew and moths when cleaned before storing	Most types can be washed — a few fragile fabrications may require dry cleaning. See Chapter 2, pg. 25.	Will curl away from the flame with slight melting and burn slowly leaving a soft black ash. It will smell like burnt hair.
Rayon **Viscose** Absorbit Fortisan Avril Zantrel Fibro	Affordable Soft "hand" — will soften more when laundered Resistant to sunlight "High wet modulus" types like Avril can be more durable	Washable but care must be taken not to stretch or weaken the fiber while wet. Can be bleached with chlorine bleach but color-test first. Press while damp to minimize wrinkling.	Will burn without a flame or melting, so doesn't leave any plastic-like residue. Light, fluffy residue. Odor will be similar to burning paper.
Cupramonnium Bemberg Cupioni	Affordable Resistant to moths and mildew Accumulates static electricity Luxurious silk-like "hand" More expensive than viscose rayon Crisper than viscose rayon Can wrinkle badly	Wash with care (see viscose rayon)	Will burn without a flame or melting, so doesn't leave any plastic-like bead. Light, fluffy residue. Odor will be similar to burning paper.

Fiber	Characteristics	Washing/Care	Burning Test
Acetate Avtex Celanese Chromspun Estron	Excellent drapability Nice in blends with stronger, more wrinkle resistant fabrics Can wrinkle excessively Weakened by direct sunlight Will dissolve in acetone (fingernail polish remover)	Can be washed with care like silk. Press while damp on wrong side to minimize wrinkling. Do not twist or wring	Flames and burns rapidly with melting, leaving a brittle, black irregular-shaped bead. The smell will be like hot vinegar (acrid).
Triacetate Arnel	Can feel "clammy" (not absorbent) Excellent color fastness Good wrinkle resistance Can be permanently pleated	A more wash and wear fiber than acetate. Quick drying — tumble or drip dry	Same as for acetate
Polyester Avlin Fortrel Dacron Kodel Encron Trevira	Can feel "clammy" (not absorbent) Wears like iron Oily stains can be difficult to get out Very wrinkle resistant Will hold a crease and/or pleat Finishes like Visa® by Milliken can improve absorbency comfort and stain removal	A wash and wear fiber Can yellow or gray if whites aren't laundered separately Pretreat greasy stains with pre-wash sprays or sticks.	Fabric will shrink away from the flame. The melting will leave a hard, gray or tan round bead. Odor will be chemical-like.
Nylon Antron Crepeset Enkalure Qiana	Very strong Can be uncomfortable to wear due to non-absorbent nature Static electricity can be a problem Qiana nylon is more absorbent, doesn't yellow, can be pressed at higher temperatures and is less static-prone than other nylons.	Same as polyester	Leaves hard, tough, gray, round bead. Odor will be like celery. *Use a match or lighter on an inconspicuous corner and be careful!

A NOTE ABOUT SYNTHETIC SILKY CARE: Avoid too hot wash water and dryers. They can permanently muss and wrinkle the fabric, cause undesirable limpness and static electricity (see pg. 25). Use a cool rinse, cooler dryer cycle or drip dry (my preference) for the most wrinkle resistance.

A Note on Knits:

Single knits have a good degree of stretch but not as much stretch or resiliency as interlocks. Interlocks are generally the stretchiest of the knits. They will run lengthwise in one direction but this can be prevented with edgestitching. Tricot knits have the most give in the crosswise rib direction but don't stretch alot. Double knits are firm and easy to sew, but less drapeable.

Whenever I go into a new fabric store my first question is: "Do you have any silk knits?" There's simply nothing more lovely than a silk or silk blend. Qiana® knits also simulate the silky look while being easy to care for and sew.

Fabric Companies and Distributors Known For Silks and Silkies:

Silks

American Silk Mills
Arthur Zeiler Fabrics
Dick and Goldschmidt
Exotic Silks
Hoffman of California
Horokoshi (through Sewing Associates)
Rimmon Silks
Rodolph Thai Silks
Roth/Unitrading
Schwarzchild Textiles
Simone's Collection
Skinner Division of Springs Mills
Utex Trading

Silkies

Blue Ridge Winkler
Gordon Fabrics (Kanebo)
Hi-Fashion Fabrics
Hoffman of California
John Kaldor Fabricmaker
Klopman Mills (Burlington)
Logantex
Rosewood Fabrics
Shirley Fabrics
Skinner Division of
  Springs Mills
South Seas Imports
Stanton-Kutasi
Thompson of California

Silk and Silk-Like Fabric Glossary

Sheer Silks and Silkies

Uses: Bias cuts, fuller garments. Use a second layer to line or underline. A sheer jacket can turn a casual garment into evening wear.

Chiffon: Plain weave, thin, very lightweight, loosely woven with highly twisted yarns.

Gauze: Loosely woven leno weave. Some are a plain weave, but they are less stable and resilient than Leno loose open weave.

Georgette: Plain weave. Fine sheer crepe made with twisted yarns so hand is crisp. Wrinkle resistant.

Organza: Plain weave. Thin sheer crisp fabric. Used for interfacings as well.

Voile: Plain weave. Soft fabric made of highly twisted yarns to lend a crisp hand.

Lightweight Silks and Silkies

Uses: Loose fitting simple garments. Soft draped styles with few seams or darts. Make a matching blouse and skirt that will look like a dress when worn together. May be layered without adding bulk.

Bouclé: Actually refers to a curled, crinkly looped or nubby yarn that when used creates a "boucle" knit or woven.

Broadcloth or Fuji: Plain weave. Soft, with dulled luster. Sometimes called shirting silk and often striped. It was originally woven in widths exceeding the usual (then) 29 inches, hence its name.

Charmeuse: Satin weave. Rich soft satin with dull back. A subdued luster due to warp twist. Drapes beautifully. Fragile.

China Silk: Plain weave. Used for linings, underlinings and lingerie. Thinner than broadcloth and can be less durable.

Crepe de chine: Plain weave. A fine, subtly lustrous fabric, with a soft drape. One of the most commonly available silks.

Crepe Back Satin: Plain weave. Light, medium and heavy weights. Heavy weights used for bridal. Satin is on right side, crepe on wrong side, but may use either side out.

Crepe Matelasse: Jacquard weave. Soft fabric with bubbly surface created in weaving.

Faille: Fine crosswise rib variation of the plain weave. Drapes well. Available in tissue to medium weights. Silk and rayon faille are rare but beautiful finds.

Habutai: Plain or twill weave. At one time produced exclusively in Japan. Similar to China Silk but heavier and more lustrous due to slight twist in the yarns. Means "soft as down" in Japanese.

Honan: Plain weave with slubbed yarns. Made from Tussah or wild silk. Often brilliantly colored or iridescent.

Lamé: Fabrics with metallic threads woven or knitted within. Often lightweight and slinky but actually can be any weight.

Pongee: Rib variation of a plain weave. Made from tussah or wild silk with a lightly textured surface. Often natural or cream colored. Many synthetic imitations.

Poplin: Rib variation of plain weave. Can also be medium weight. Tightly woven dense fabric with fine ribs formed by heavier filling yarns.

Surah: Twill weave. Distinctive diagonal ribs.-Often printed or plaid.

Tissue: Light weight version of silky fabrics like faille, crepe and taffeta.

19

Medium to Suitweight Silks and Silkies

Uses: Oriental inspired looks, quilted and patchwork styles. Simple tailored lines for heavier weights.

Bengaline (or grosgrain): Rib variation of plain weave. Rib runs in a crosswise direction. Heavier than faille. Grosgrain is ribbon width bengaline. First made in Bengal, India.

Brocade: Jacquard weave all over design. Solid or multi-colored often with metallic threads running throughout.

Crepe: Plain weave. Medium and also made in light weight. Has crinkled surface texture due to highly twisted yarns, chemical treatments, weaving and/or embossing.

Damask: Jacquard weave. Elaborate patterns woven into the fabric — can be reversible.

Moiré: An embossed finish applied to ribbed fabrics like faille, taffeta and bengaline. Fabrics are subjected to heat and pressure to give a wavy, watered, effect to the surface. Generally medium weight, but also can be light and heavy.

Ottoman: Rib variation of plain weave. A fabric with a heavy, widely spaced crosswise rib. The filling rib yarn may be varied because the warp covers the filling entirely.

Peau de soie. Rib variation of plain weave so fine that it gives a satiny face. Weights will vary, but can be quite heavy. Strong, firm fabric with dull satiny surface. In French it means "skin of silk."

Shantung: Rib variation of plain weave. When silk, slubbed effect from duppioni yarns. Heavier than pongee. Name derived from Shantung, a Chinese province. Generally medium weight. Constructed to look like flax linen. Many synthetic imitations.

Taffeta: Plain weave. Can be any weight, but generally medium weight. Crisp hand. Rustles (called scroop) when crushed or rubbed together.

Velvet: Plain weave pile fabric. Silk velvet is gorgeous but uncommon. Rayon velvet is its replacement. Can be brocaded. Panne velvet is knit or woven with the pile flattened for a very slinky look and hand. Figured or patterned velvet can be created by cutting the pile or by the burn-out print method.

CHAPTER THREE
Yes, You Can Wash Silk

Take it from me, I wouldn't even own silks if I couldn't wash them. I have a baby (that urps), two dogs (that jump on me), peacocks (that make a *big* mess) and a 200 acre farm.

Water is used throughout the silk making process, both to loosen the fiber from the cocoon and then to remove the gummy sericin. Water actually refreshes the silk fiber. I prefer the look, feel, and smell of my silk blouses when they are washed. I *don't* wash loosely woven or fragile fabrics or suits because of all the inner construction.

Ensure Washability by Sewing Your Own Silks

The best reason to sew your own silk garments is that by prewashing the ingredients you can then wash the finished garment. "Dry clean only" labels are used by ready-to-wear manufacturers because they can't prewash fabric, linings and interfacings. The label also protects manufacturers from the wrath of consumers who throw silks in the hot wash cycle with blue jeans!

Preshrinking Silk Yardage — Wet to Dry in 5 Minutes!

1. Use the bathroom sink for smaller pieces, the bathtub for larger pieces.

2. Draw lukewarm water and add a mild liquid detergent like dishwashing types.

3. Place folded fabric in the water and swish the fabric around 1-2 minutes.

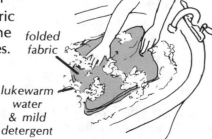

folded fabric

lukewarm water & mild detergent

4. Rinse thoroughly in cool water.

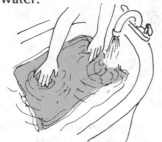

5. Lay the wet fabric on a towel and roll up to blot out the excess moisture.

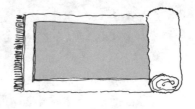

6. Using a dry or steam iron at a low steam setting, iron the fabric dry. VOILA! The fabric is ready to be cut, sewn, worn, and washed again.

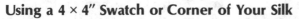

Test BEFORE Preshrinking

Using a 4 × 4″ Swatch or Corner of Your Silk

Most silks *can* be handwashed, but four qualities can change. Prewashing a test sample will help you decide whether or not the changes bother you. Wash and iron dry as in preshrinking.

1. **Color** — Virtually all silks and most silk blends lose some color in washing. It is not fading, but a run-off of excess dye. You will notice the greatest color change in intense or brightly colored silks. They will stay brightest if dry cleaned. I wash mine anyway. Prints can also be washed — your test sample will tell you if there is permanent running of darker colors onto light. Most importantly, do *you* like the color of the washed and dried sample?

2. **Texture** — Some silks get a little stiffer, some a little softer, and some a little crepier. Do you like the textural change?

3. **Sheen** — Some surfaces will become duller after washing. How does the sample look?

4. **Size** — Some types of silk will shrink more than others. If you bought 3 yards for a dress and lost ¼ yard in preshrinking, you may not have enough for the dress. I'm 5′ 10″ so

I always buy ⅛ yard per yard extra to allow for shrinkage. A quick way to see how much length you'll lose is to measure the 4 × 4″ square after pre-shrinking. Mark the crosswise and lengthwise grain directions. 4″ is ⅑th of a yard. If your 4 × 4″ square shrinks ¼″ in length, that would be ¼″ × 9 or 2¼″ per yard. Will you have enough fabric?

size after shrinkage

lengthwise

4″

4″

¼″ shrinkage →

Some silks are too fragile, will lose their sheen, or shrink excessively if washed. Bill Brandt from American Silk Mills recommends dry cleaning for silk brocades, chiffon, some crepes, metallics, taffeta, satin and charmeuse.

Caring For Silk Garments

1. **Don't wait too long between washings.** Wash your garments frequently so they will come clean without using heavily concentrated detergents or prolonged soaking. Also, moths won't attack clean silk.

2. **Wash the garment in the same way the yardage was prewashed.** The key to success . . . only wash when you have time to press too. If you press the fabric while it is still wet or damp it will dry instantly and wrinkle-free.

3. **Use your sleeve board** to press sleeves and small detail areas.

4. **A looser fit** means less wrinkling.

5. **Use fatter hangers.** Padded or plastic hangers are best for silk garments. Thin wire hangers don't provide enough support and fading and wear lines can occur along the wire.

6. **Wear dress shields** to minimize stains and frequency of washing. Dress shields will protect your silk from harmful effects of aluminum hydrochloride, the chemical in most anti-perspirants (it does more damage than the perspiration itself).

Answers to Frequently Asked Silk Care Questions

1. What's the best water temperature for washing silks?
Lukewarm water (100°F) is best for removing soil and body oils. Cold water (50°F) is best for rinsing. It will remove soap and will also minimize wrinkling. Rinse thoroughly.

23

2. Is it better to use soap or detergents?

Mild detergents are universally better than soaps because they work in all water types, but in soft water areas, Ivory Snow and other soaps are fine. I've successfully used Woolite, Wool Tone® by Van Wyck, and the least expensive liquid dishwashing detergents. Shampoos are mild detergents and I use them often when traveling, but they are expensive and contain unnecessary conditioners. Heavy duty laundry detergents contain builders that can be harmful to silk if used frequently, but may be necessary in removing "ring around the collar."

3. Should I use bleach on silks?

NEVER USE CHLORINE BLEACH on silk. It will cause permanent damage to the fiber. However, liquid hydrogen peroxide or dry oxygen type bleaches called "all-fabric" bleaches like Clorox II can be used. Avoid enzyme bleaches. Always *test* first on a hidden corner or seam allowance. Do not bleach just a stained area — it can cause lightening of just the spot. Add bleach to the wash water, following the package instructions.

4. Can I machine wash and dry silk? Line dry?

When washing by machine, set on the short delicate cycle. Actually, a washing machine tub can work better than a sink for large garments or lots of yardage because the extra water held in the large tub will help dilute the dye run-off. Don't wash your silks with other garments or fabrics that could pick up excess dye. Protect a small delicate silk garment by putting it in a mesh bag before machine washing.

When drying it's better to "press dry" silks. They will be wrinkle-free and softer. Don't line dry in direct sunlight. It will weaken the fiber.

5. What can I do about static electricity?

Some options: a) Spray either the wrong side of the silk or your pantyhose or slip with Static Guard™ or a similar product. b) Use a fabric softener when washing your silk, your lingerie, and/or your pantyhose. c) An emergency measure that works temporarily is to wipe your pantyhose, slip or legs with a damp paper towel. Water prevents cling.

6. Do I need to preshrink silks that I plan to dry clean?
    Steam pressing the yardage before cutting will take care of most shrinkage caused when the dry cleaner presses. I often will prewash my silks even when I plan to dry clean. It eliminates water spotting and then I can wash the garment if I need to, particularly when traveling.

NOTE: Saavy seamsters prewash interfacings, other shaping fabrics (see pg. 34) and notions to ensure washability and dry cleaning success.

7. What about spots and stains?
    Some should be removed by a professional dry cleaner. Some can be treated at home. The longer any stain sets the harder it is to remove. Consult your cleaner as soon as possible when spots and stains occur and/or if your garment has not been pre-shrunk. Always test any home removal method first on an inconspicuous corner. Never rub silk as rubbing abrades the surface and creates light spots.

Water spots — If you've preshrunk your silk, you will not have problems with water spots. Your entire garment becomes one big water spot! For garments not preshrunk, have your dry cleaner remove the water spot.

Oil and Grease — If you catch the spot immediately, and your fabric has been prewashed, treat it directly with mild liquid detergent. Allow the detergent to sit a couple minutes, then rinse.
OR — try cleaning solvents like Carbona, Energine, and prewash spotting sprays, but follow package directions and *test* on an inconspicuous area as they can remove dyes.

Blood, coffee, cocoa — Dilute the stain immediately with cold water and then wash.

Ink — Try using vinegar, but test first. Ink may fade through repeated washings.

Perfume — The alcohol base in perfumes weakens silk and causes dyes to fade. Never put perfume directly on or next to the silk.

NOTE: If you are regularly washing all silk garments, but a few stubborn stains remain, have them dry cleaned occasionally. Chances are the stains will disappear!

NOTE: For silky synthetic fabric care, see pgs. 16-17.

CHAPTER FOUR

Coordinating Pattern and Fabric

Silks and silkies seem to flatter just about any figure, skimming body contours without clinging. The lighter weight types can be gathered and pleated without being bulky or "poufy." You may be able to wear fashion looks you thought never possible. I've always avoided dirndl skirts due to my basic pear shape, but in drapable lightweight silks and silkies the waistline gathers fall softly adding neither weight nor unnecessary fullness to my ample hips.

And don't be afraid to layer the silks and silkies. Several silky layers don't add weight or bulk like other fabrics and can actually camouflage figure flaws (a tip I picked up from **Sew Big** by Palmer/Pletsch author, Marilyn Thelen). Go ahead — wear a blouse over a camisole, all tucked into a dirndl skirt. In silkies the look can be surprisingly slenderizing.

Whenever possible, make a skirt out of the same fabric as a silk or silk-like blouse. The look can be worn as a dress or separates — a real wardrobe extender.

Where to Start

1. **Try on ready to wear.** You'll get great ideas on which silk and silky fabrics work best for different silhouettes and how they look on your figure. Since there's now a pattern for just about every fashion look it will make deciding on flattering styles really easy.

2. **Study the pattern catalogue.** You'll see that many of the current styles are photographed in silks and silkies (they make even the simplest styles look lovely). Under "fabrics" on the back of the pattern envelope look for silk and silk-like fabrications (Chapter 2, pgs. 18-20).

27

3. **Drape the fabric** on your body simulating the prospective pattern style. How does the fabric drape? Try pleating, blousing, and gathering the fabric, creating the neckline and whatever the details are in your pattern. Draping takes some of the guesswork out of coordinating pattern and fabric and we so often forget how easy it is.

What to Look For in a Pattern

1. **Less detail.** Pleats, tucks, and ruffles (see Chapter 13, pg. 71) can be gorgeous but certainly aren't essential to creating a gorgeous garment! Remember that "less can be beautiful" when it comes to silks and silkies.

2. **Looser Fit.** You'll notice that silky styles are usually looser fitting. This is an important factor to keep in mind when choosing a pattern for the more fragile lightweight silks and silkies. Because of their characteristic drape you don't need as many seams, darts and fitting lines. A too-tight fit can put undo strain on seams and create a wrinkling problem. Choose more tailored, fitted styles for heavier weight fabric types.

Understanding Ease

Patterns are designed with built-in comfort — a feature known as "wearing ease." Wearing ease is the extra fullness added to a pattern so that you can move, sit, walk, lift comfortably. Depending on the garment style there may also be additional ease added called "design ease." It determines the silhouette and fashion look.

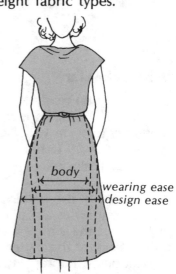

body

wearing ease
design ease

28

One guideline for the amount of design ease in a pattern is the style description on the back of the pattern. Generally I stick with styles that are described as "loose-fitting" or "semi-fitted" for lightweight silks and silkies. Run down the list on pages 13 & 14 to determine if your fabric will perform well in this pattern style.

Try on the Tissue Pattern

To determine how the design looks on you and how much ease it has, pin the pattern tissue together and try it on. Remember, you will want more than minimal wearing ease for most silks and silkies. It's wise to add 1" side seam allowances so seams can be let out if necessary.

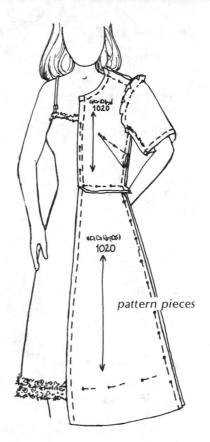

pattern pieces

The No-Fail Pattern/Fabric Chart

Choose styles and fabrics from the respective easy, easier, and easiest, categories keeping your sewing talents and time restrictions in mind. Even if you're a beginner, selecting styles and fabrics from the "easiest" category should prove to be nearly goof-proof. No matter what your sewing expertise, it's better to make an "easiest" style well than a more specialized "easy" style poorly. I made a sheer silk pullover blouse, elegantly dressy and so easy in just 2 hours.

You can't get too much of a good thing, so once you've found a style and fabric that work well for you, sew them time and time again. I have made the same v-neck "t-shirt" style blouse in several colors and prints.

Pattern Design

Easy

Silhouette
semi-fitted and fitted,
fitted tailored looks for
medium to heavier
silks and silkies

Edge Finishes
piping

Sleeves
set in with placket and
cuff, pleated sleeve
cap, French cuffs,
shoulder pads/cap
shapers

Other Design Details
pleats and tucks,
ruffles, bias lines,
bound or handworked
buttonholes, lining-
underlining, collar and
stand, jacket tailoring

Fabrics

Sheer
chiffon

Lightweight
very lightweight
velvets, crepe
matellasse

Medium to Heavier
Weight
taffeta, Shantung,
slipper satin, Damask

Pattern Design

Easier

Silhouette
loosely fitted and semi-fitted

Edge Finishes
bound, hemmed, faced, simple skirt waistbands

Sleeves
set-in with Painless Placket and cuff (see Chapter 18, pg. 99).

Other Design Details
zipper closures, collars, simple ties, drawstrings machine buttonholes, hidden button placket, cardigan styled jackets

Fabrics

Sheer
organza, voile, georgette, sheer tricot

Lightweight
crepe, crepe-backed satin, China silk, pongee, poplin, charmeuse

Medium to Heavier Weight
ottoman, bengaline brocade, peau de soie, matellesse, moire, panne velvet

Pattern Design

Easiest

Fabrics

Pattern Design

NOTE: look in the "easy" sections of the pattern catalogue

Silhouette
very loose and loose fitting, "adjustable" fit wrap tops and skirts

Edge Finishes
faced necklines, machine-stitched edges

Sleeves
raglan, simple set in, dolman, capped, hemmed-no cuffs

Other Design Details
(or lack thereof) no darts or buttons, elastics and simple drawstrings

Fabrics

Lightweight
crepe de chine, broadcloth, faille, honan, surah

Knits
all types, especially interlocks, lightweight double knits

CHAPTER FIVE

Shaping Fabrics for Silks and Silkies

However subtle, shaping fabrics can make or break even the softest fashions. Of course in tailored styles, they're a must. In softer fashions they can be minimized or occasionally eliminated. Here are some of the possible shaping layers used in silky silhouettes:

Underlining: A soft or self-fabric layer that provides shape, body, and support, and is sewn into garment seams. For example, a straight skirt or pant can be underlined for strength and wrinkle resistance. A bodice may be underlined for modesty — the sleeves can be left single layer.

Interfacing: A stabilizing layer that is used to prevent stretching and add body to garment edges and detail areas like collars, cuffs, and closures. In sheers and lightweights, this layer may be self-fabric or very lightweight interfacing fabric.

Lining: Usually a slippery fabric layer cut and sewn separately from the fashion fabric and joined at the waistband, facings, etc. It allows jackets to be easily slipped on and off and covers inside construction. And lining also helps prevent bagging in the seat area.

There are some styles that do not require shapers . . . particularly if made of fabrics with body that are bound, piped or edge stitched (see Chapters 15, 16 and 22). The edging treatment works to shape, stabilize and strengthen edges and/or hems.

Interfacings — Fusibles vs. Stitchables

The key to interfacing success is *testing* — both fusibles and stitchables:

Testing Fusibles:
Cut 2″ × 2″ (or so) squares of fusible options — try two or three different types and colors. Fuse to a scrap of the fashion fabric following manufacturer's instructions. If you will be washing the finished garment, wash the test sample and press. If dry cleaning, leave as is. Then ask the following questions:

Testing Stitchables:
Place the fashion fabric together with your interfacing. Sandwiching one layer of interfacing between two layers of fashion fabric usually simulates garment layers best. Feel them. Then ask the following questions:

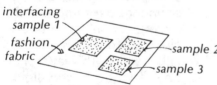

interfacing sample 1
fashion fabric
sample 2
sample 3

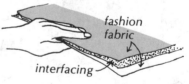

fashion fabric
interfacing

• How do the fabrics feel together? Does the interfacing give your fabric enough body — or too much? Fusibles have more body after fusing, stitchables soften with wear and laundering.

• Look at the right side of the fabric — is there a color change? Are there lumps, bubbles or spots? This could mean you are using the wrong interfacing or haven't followed proper fusing instructions.

• Do the fabrics and interfacing have compatible care requirements?

• Is the interfacing "give" appropriate to your fabric and pattern? Use the "give" direction (multi-directional or cross-wise in non-wovens, bias in wovens) to create supple, rolled shaping in collars, cuffs, etc. The stable direction prevents stretching in buttonholes, waistbands, plackets, pockets, etc.

• Does the interfacing change the fabric color? Put a layer of interfacing between two layers of garment fabric and hold it up to your skin.

If the interfacing shows through too much, choose a color closer to your skin tone. The lingerie guideline that "skin-colored underwear shows the least" applies here.

Fusibles Are Particularly Nice on These Fabrics

1. **Interlock and single knit silks and silkies** — I like non-wovens like Sheer Weight Fusible Pellon® 906F or Armo's So Sheer™, used on the facings only or small detail areas like the upper collar and upper cuff.

2. **Lightweight silks and silkies** like crepe de chine, faille, poplin and broadcloth. Hoorah! There's finally an interfacing that works! Stacy's Easy-Knit® seems to be perfect for light-weight silks and silky wovens. It won't pucker after washing.

Use Stitchables Only For These Fabrics

• **Silky sheers** — fusibles can "strike through" to the right side.

• **Nubby or napped surface textures** like velvets, matel-lesses, very crinkly crepes — that can be crushed by the fusing pressure and heat.

• **Lamé** — some silkies that have a high metallic content also have a very low melting point.

• **Triacetates** — fusibles may not adhere to fabrics with a high traicetate fiber content.

Fashion Fabric

	Sheers	Lightweight
Fusible Interfacing	Usually not recommended — test first (see fusibles for lightweights)	Sheer Weight Fusible Pellon® 906F SoSheer™ by Armo Lightweight Easy-Shaper® by Stacy Easy-Knit® by Stacy
Stitchable Interfacing	Sheer Weight Sew-In Pellon® 905 Silk organza Self-fabric	Sheer Weight Sew-In Pellon® 905 Armo-Press® Soft Poly SiBonne Plus by Armo Silk organza Self-fabric
Underlining	Usually not required — self-fabric can be elegant if not too crisp Poly SiBonne Plus Lining fabrics	Self-fabric China Silk Poly-SiBonne Plus by Armo
Lining	China Silk Tissue faille Ciao!™ by Armo Poly SiBonne Plus by Armo Butterfly® by Stacy Most slippery, lightweight silks or silkies can be used.	China Silk Tissue faille Ciao!™ by Armo Butterfly® by Stacy Slippery fabrics in this same weight category can also be used

Medium Weight	Suitings	Knits
Sof-Shape® Pellon® 880F Sure-Fuse™ by Stacy Featherweight Fusible Pellon® 911FF Shape-Flex® All-purpose by Stacy	Pel-Aire® by Pellon 881F Tailor's Touch™ by Stacy Suit Shape® by Stacy Armo Weft by Armo Suitweight Easy-Shaper® by Stacy Easy-Knit® by Stacy	Sof-Shape® by Pellon Sheer Weight Fusible Pellon® 906F Easy-Shaper® Lightweight by Stacy Easy-Knit® by Stacy Using knit fusibles on knit fabrics can cause skipped stitches. TEST first.
Add-Shape™ Medium Lite by Stacy Featherweight Sew-In Pellon® 910 Veriform Durable Press and Sta-Shape® Durable Press by Stacy	ArmoPress Firm Fino II (P-I) by Armo Any good goat hair interfacing	Fusibles are recommended for most knits
China Silk Poly SiBonne Plus	China Silk Poly SiBonne Plus	Self-fabric when needed Lightweight nylon tricot
China Silk Tissue faille Ciao!™ by Armo Butterfly® by Stacy Slippery lightweight silks and silkies like Ultressea and Coupe de Ville from Burlington/Klopman, Lutesong, A la Creme and Palazzio by Skinner. Polyester linings	Medium weight and suitings have same lining requirements	No lining usually required

How To Fuse — The Steps:

1. Warm your fashion fabric by pressing with steam. This removes any wrinkles or remaining shrinkage.

2. Place your interfacing resin side down on the fabric.

3. Hold the iron 2" above the interfacing and steam for three-four seconds to remove any residual shrinkage.

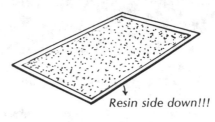

Resin side down!!!

4. Now press "baste" lightly from the center to the outside edge.

5. Fuse the two layers together following manufacturer's instructions, always using a press cloth to protect your fabric from the iron temperature. Use a wool setting with steam. Lightweight fabrics usually only need about 10 seconds, heavier weight, 12-15 seconds in each spot. Be sure to fuse for the *full count* or the fusible will be under-fused and eventually separate from the fabric.

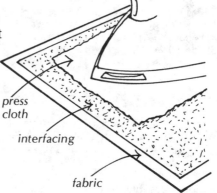

press cloth

interfacing

fabric

Where to Fuse:

A good goof-proof policy is to fuse interfacings only to the facings, under collars and under cuffs. Then any texture change or strike through will be on an inside layer. When using lightweight fusibles you won't need to trim the interfacing before fusing . . . just layer the seam allowance to minimize bulk.

under-cuff

undercollar

Remember that more than one interfacing may be necessary in a garment. For example, I often fuse to the upper collar and cuffs of lightweight silks and silkies to prevent the seam allowance ridge around the edges from showing. Easy-Knit® seems to work the best, but always test first! It fuses smoothly and won't bubble after washing.

However, Easy-Knit® is stretchy, so in a blouse I use woven sew-in interfacing or self fabric down the front for more stability.

On the facing of a V-neck dress or blouse made of lightweight fabric I prefer lightweight non-woven fusible like Sheer Weight Fusible Pellon® 906F fused to the facing. (The non-wovens are more stable than knits like Easy-Knit®). If bubbling does occur, it's not a problem since it won't show on the garment.

NOTE: On heavier fabrics, trim ½" off the edge of fusibles interfacing before fusing to eliminate bulk.

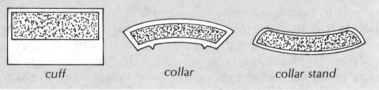

| cuff | collar | collar stand |

How to Use Stitchables — The Steps:

Glue interfacings in place! Use flexible craft glue like Slomon's SOBO found in most notion departments. Glue on seam allowances only since this glue will not wash out.

' 1. Press the fabric and interfacing pieces together to remove any wrinkles.

2. Sparingly dot glue along outer edges of the seam allowances. Pat together. To get a fine line of SOBO, twist the nozzle only about a quarter turn.

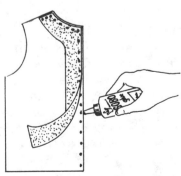

3. Allow five minutes for drying.

Where to Use Stitchables

Glue baste the interfacing to the garment rather than facings along the seam allowance edges. Stitchable interfacings are not pre-trimmed. Trim and grade after stitching the seam.

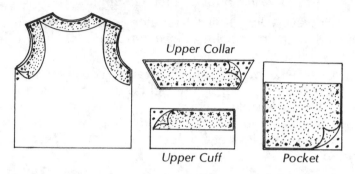

Upper Collar

Upper Cuff   Pocket

Stock Up Your Interfacing Store

Don't dampen your sewing spirits by having to make a special trip to the store for interfacings! Pick two or three interfacings and underlinings out of those categories you are more inclined to sew (see pgs. 36 & 37). Buy three yards of each — all-store sales are a good time to stock up. Pre-shrink all at once to minimize the time spent per garment.

Preshrinking Before Testing

To get realistic test results, you must pre-shrink both your fabric and interfacings, and other shaping layers. Follow our preshrinking instructions for silks and silkies in Chapter 3, pg. 21.

Why? Ugly bubbling or pulling can be caused by either or both the fabric or fusible interfacing shrinking. Have you noticed how many readymades have this problem after laundering? A real advantage to sewing is that you can pretreat and put an end to these disasters. Underlinings must be pre-shrunk to prevent pulling on the seamlines, poor drape and fit. I only preshrink linings if the garment will be washed . . . most lined garments are dry cleaned instead.

Preshrinking Fusibles

• Wovens and knits: Place in a basin of HOT water. Don't worry, it will not hurt the fusing agent which is activated by temperatures of 300°F+! Soak for about 20 minutes. Do not wad, wring or throw into the dryer (agitation could dislodge the fusing agent). Instead, roll in a towel to remove the excess water. Then hang over a shower curtain rod or towel rack to dry.

• Non-wovens (generally shrink less than wovens or knits): You will need an iron that steams well. Put a press cloth on your ironing surface. Place the interfacing resin side down on the press cloth. Hold your iron 2" above the interfacing and steam for three-four seconds in each area. You'll actually see some interfacings shrink while steaming (continue until they don't shrink anymore).

Preshrinking Stitchables

Non-woven stitchables have virtually no shrinkage factor, so preshrinking is unnecessary. For woven stitchables:

• For dry clean only garments: Follow the directions for pre-shrinking woven and knit fusibles.

• For washable garments: Pre-wash and dry as you would the finished garment.

Underlining is Also A "Glueable"

The "glue and fold" method described in **Mother Pletsch's Painless Sewing** is a favorite of mine. This method makes the underlining slightly smaller to allow for inner layer "take-up".

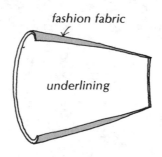

fashion fabric

underlining

CHAPTER SIX
‌‌Threads, Pins, Needles

Thread — You Don't Have to Use Silk for Silkies

Friends have told me that they couldn't sew on silk because they couldn't find silk thread! Forget that notion. I've used all types of threads successfully on silks, from silk to cotton . . . don't take thread (or any notion for that matter) too seriously. Here are a few guidelines:

TEST. Just sew some test seams on your fabric. Check for stitch quality and length. Pull on the seam to see if the thread will cut the fabric or break too easily, especially on knits. If thread continually breaks and frays away from the machine needle, its diameter may be too large for the needle eye. Change to a larger needle.

• I like lingerie-type threads, like Coats & Clark Dual Duty Plus® Extra Fine for silk and silkies.

• Silk thread comes in very fine diameters but is extremely strong and can actually "cut" seams in a fitted garment. In looser fitting garments it works well (if you can find it).

• Polyester or polyester core/cotton wrapped threads are the most commonly available and suitable for most silky sewing, both knits and wovens. There are many different types of polyester and poly/cotton threads to choose from today — from long staple imported polyesters like Guterman® and Metrosene® (these tend to be a bit finer), to readily available domestic threads. Test to determine which ones work best with your fabric and machine. Don't skimp on polyester thread quality. Unbranded bargain types can be poor quality and drive you crazy!

• Some of the silk companies we work with recommend 100% cotton thread because cotton is weaker than the fabric and it "cuts" the fabric less. Also, some machines seem to stitch more evenly and smoothly with cotton thread. If you have trouble finding it, ask at sewing machine dealerships and in quilting shops.

• Most topstitching on lighter weight silks is done with regular sewing thread. For heavier weight silkies, use topstitching thread (silk, polyester or cotton). A size 18 needle will have to be used with some of the very heavy threads — but other topstitching threads can be sewn with a size 14 or 16 needle *TEST!*

The Pin and Needle Basics

For silks and silkies, correct size and good condition are important. Coordinate the size to your fabric and thread through testing and throw away any blunt or rusted tips! Damaged pins and needles can snag and make holes in the delicate surfaces.

• Pins range in length and come in both ball (best for knits) and sharp (best for wovens) points. Generally the larger the size, the longer the pin and the larger the diameter (16-20 sizes the most common). See how susceptible your fabric is to pin holes and snagging through testing. Special fabric may require a new box of pins, but in general you'll be well-equipped with your pin hodge-podge minus blunt tips and rusted types.

• "Silk" pins aren't really the finest pins available. For lighter weight and delicate surface silkies use pleating or extra-fine pleating pins. Stainless steel pins are best . . . they don't rust.

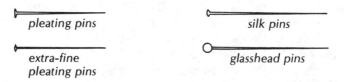

pleating pins

silk pins

extra-fine
pleating pins

glasshead pins

• I still find long (1¼"+) pins with large glass or colored heads the easiest to use, but they aren't fine.

Hand Needles

Any one of these can be used for silky sewing, although sharps are most common. A good rule of thumb is the longer the stitch, the longer the needle you'll need.

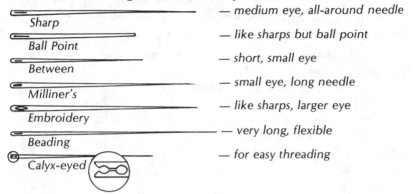

Sharp — medium eye, all-around needle

Ball Point — like sharps but ball point

Between — short, small eye

Milliner's — small eye, long needle

Embroidery — like sharps, larger eye

Beading — very long, flexible

Calyx-eyed — for easy threading

Needles are available in sizes 1-10. Size 10 is finest and best for most hand sewing, particularly "The Perfectly Invisible Hem" (see pg. 125). When you find a package of all size 10 sharps, buy them!

Embroidery needles are better if you have trouble threading the needle because the eye is longer. The finer the needle, the smaller the eye. A needle threader can help with the smaller eye sizes.

Machine Needles

The wrong sewing machine needle can ruin a silky fabric project. For most silky fabrics, machine needle sizes 9-11 (European 65-75) are suitable, but . . . TEST! The needle should be small enough to pierce the fabric without leaving a hole, but large enough for the thread to pass with accurate tension.

U.S. SIZES		EUROPEAN SIZES
9/10	fine	65/70
11/12	fine	75/80
14	medium	90
16	coarse	100
18	coarse	110

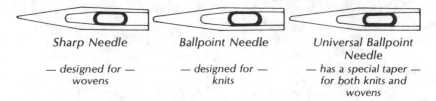

Sharp Needle	Ballpoint Needle	Universal Ballpoint Needle
— designed for — wovens	— designed for — knits	— has a special taper — for both knits and wovens

A good general rule is to use a new needle for every new silky garment. Be prepared to change needles as the stitch quality or fabric can be effected by a dulled or damaged needle. And always after stitching into a pin!

And what about Singer* Yellow and Red Band Needles? These needles have a longer "scarf" so the top thread forms a larger thread loop and the hook of the bobbin can get closer to the needle. The result? Elimination of skipped stitches. Try the Yellow Band ball point — now available in sizes 9-16 and the Red Band sharp point comes in sizes 11-16.

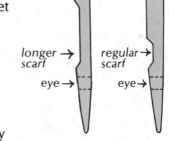

longer → scarf

eye →

regular → scarf

eye →

*Trademark of the Singer Company

Keeping Needle Sizes Categorized

Some people are organized enough to put a reusable machine needle back into the appropriate package. I'm not. Since my husband's logger jeans are mended in between sewing a sheer silk blouse, I'm frequently changing needles and need to keep track of sizes.

The best method I've found is to purchase several inexpensive small pin cushions and label them with pen as to "size 9-11 ball point," "size 9-11 Yellow Band," etc. Then I just stick the needles in the appropriate cushion.

How do you remember what size and type needle is in the machine? Sew into a small scrap of your fabric before getting up from the machine. When you return you'll know the needle size and type plus thread adaptability.

CHAPTER SEVEN

Cutting and Marking

Since silks and silkies are just that — silky and slippery — they present a few more cutting challenges. Marking can be tricky only because some surfaces are particularly delicate and/or sheer.

Cutting Tips for Silky Fabrics

• Pre-shrink (see Chapter 3, pgs. 21-23) before cutting your fabric and shaping fabrics.

• To straighten fabric ends, either tear or cut along the crosswise grain. I've found that many better fabric stores do tear lightweight, plain weave silks and silk types, but this can cause pulling along the edge of certain fabrics . . . a problem if you're short on yardage. If so, pull a thread and cut along it to straighten. Heavier weight silkies can usually be "eye-balled" to straighten . . . or raveled to one continuous crosswise thread.

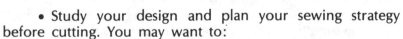

pull a thread

• Study your design and plan your sewing strategy before cutting. You may want to:
— Create "Marta's Painless Sleeve Placket" (see pg. 99).
— Cut all seams 1" wide (I always do) for easy seam finishing and "fitting insurance."
— Eliminate a seam line that is on straight of grain by placing it on the fold.

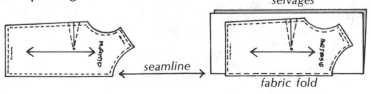

selvages

seamline

fabric fold

— "Cut-on" pockets in lightweight fabrics if yardage allows.

— Cut straight seams on the selvage to eliminate seam finishing. Clip into selvages if they pucker after laundering.
— Extend facing width to make a "cut-on self-inter-faced" facing (see pg. 94).
— Cut pattern pieces on the bias like sleeves, cuffs, ties, collars, etc. to take advantage of the diagonal "give" and design lines (see Chapter 14, pg. 79).
— Line to the edge and eliminate facings.

• Pin the pattern to your fabric. Long glass head pins work well. If they are stabbed vertically into your cutting board and angled toward the center of each piece, as shown, they will minimize slippage and you'll need fewer pins.

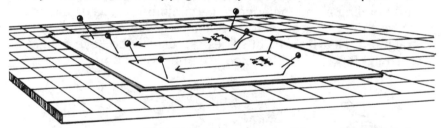

• If you are still having a slippage problem, pin the fabric to tissue paper or plain newsprint. Fold the fabric for the layout and pin to the paper. Then position and pin the pattern pieces through all layers. If the fabric has been folded right sides together, the tissue can be sewn right into the seams later for easier stitching and then torn away.

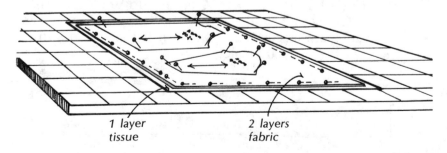

1 layer
tissue

2 layers
fabric

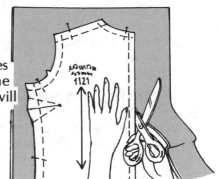

• Cut in long, even strokes holding the pattern flat with one hand, close to the edges. This will minimize the number of pins required to control the fabric.

• Cut nubby, heavier weight silkies single layer if they have a tendency to stick together. Or, put a layer of tissue between the two layers to keep them from sticking.

• Some satin surfaces may have a nap because the surface luster can cause shading. If so, cut all pattern pieces in one direction, as shown in the "with nap" layouts on the guide sheet.

• Watch for permanent crease or soil lines along the fabric fold, especially on knits. Create new fold lines by refolding the fabric, keeping the selvage edges parallel.

• Interlock knits run in one direction . . . figure out what that direction is by stretching either end of the yardage on the crosswise grain. Position pattern hemlines so the hemlines run "up." Staystitching will prevent running.

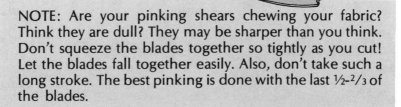

• Our ultimate "quick 'n dirty" tip — cut alongside shoulder, center front and back seams, side seams, and hemlines with pinking shears — saves you from doing it later! The inside point of the pinking is your edge for gauging standard seam width.

NOTE: Are your pinking shears chewing your fabric? Think they are dull? They may be sharper than you think. Don't squeeze the blades together so tightly as you cut! Let the blades fall together easily. Also, don't take such a long stroke. The best pinking is done with the last ½-2/3 of the blades.

• Don't let your fabric hang off the cutting board or your table while cutting. This could pull the fabric off grain, resulting in poor garment fit, drape and durability.

Marking

• Silkies are delicate and when it comes to marking — less is better. Try snip and press marking (see below), then pin marking, before resorting to markers or tracing paper. Mark wrong sides with Scotch® Brand Magic Transparent® Tape.

• Transfer all construction symbols with super fast "snip markings". Cut off notches and snip ¼" into seam allowances. Dots and fold lines can also be marked with snips.

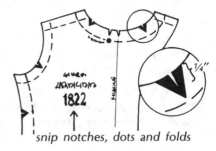

snip notches, dots and folds

• "Press marking" can be done while the pattern is still pinned to the fabric. Use it to lightly mark center front fold lines, pleats, tucks, etc. (For more information on pleat and tuck marking, see pg. 71).

• Pin marking, in combination with snipping and pressing is still my favorite and the safest marking method. For marking, use pins with small heads — they rip the pattern less. Folding your fabric right sides together will also make the pin marking easier. Stick the pins through all layers from both sides — start with the pattern side first. Separate the layers carefully and secure the pins by sticking the points back into the fabric.

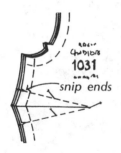

snip ends

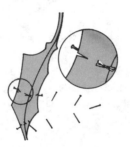

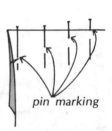

pin marking

• When these fast marking methods aren't adequate, try using a smooth edge tracing wheel — with or without tracing paper. The indentations made by the wheel may be enough marking. The new washable tracing papers like Trace-B-Gone™ by Dritz® are recommended but they don't make as distinguishable a mark as the old papers. To allow you to mark harder without ruining your pattern, try this Palmer/Pletsch seminar tip: Place a lightweight sandwich bag on top of your pattern while using the tracing wheel. Your pattern will last a lot longer.

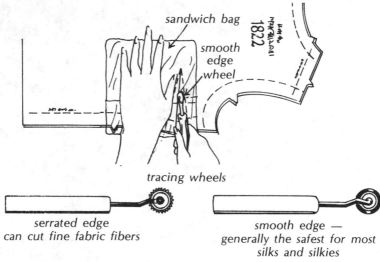

sandwich bag

smooth
edge
wheel

tracing wheels

serrated edge
can cut fine fabric fibers

smooth edge —
generally the safest for most
silks and silkies

• Washable marking pens like Wonder Marker™ or Mark-B-gone™ can be used on washable fabrics. The marks should come out with cool water. There are some marking pens available now that are advertised to "disappear (the markings!) in 48 hours." But as a fail-safe policy, always test removability of these marks.

• On dry-clean only fabrics, use tailor's chalk (I like chalk pencils) or tailor's tacks if pin, snip and press markings won't suffice (most of the time they will). For long darts, I pin mark, then use a tailor's chalk pencil . . . this can help prevent sewing on pins.

CHAPTER EIGHT
Sewing on Slippery Fabrics

You and your machine should have no particular difficulties sewing medium to heavyweight silks. The slippery, lighter weight silkies can present some sewing problems. But once you've read through all the possible solutions in this chapter, sewing silkies will be easy on any type or vintage machine.

But I must remind you again *TEST*. The few minutes you spend experimenting with types of thread, needles, machine adjustments and stitching techniques on scrap fabric will save hours of frustration later. Believe me, I never spend more than 15 minutes testing.

> NOTE: All the problems listed below can be at least partially solved with a clean, lint-free and oiled machine and a new needle. *ALWAYS*, clean away all oil before sewing silkies. See your machine manual for more details. If it's been awhile, it may need professional servicing. Also, change to a machine foot with a flat bottom surface. They are excellent for lightweight silkies because the fabric is held taut under the foot.

If you run into problems, here are some solutions:

The Silky Sewing Troubleshooter.

PROBLEM: Your machine is "eating the silky fabric."

SOLUTIONS:

• Change to a small round hole plate for all straight stitching, or cover a wider zigzag hole with Scotch® Brand Magic Transparent® Tape. When the needle goes through the tape it will form a small hole. CAUTION: Change back to a larger hole plate when zigzagging.

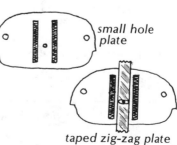

small hole plate

taped zig-zag plate

• Start stitching right at the edge of the fabric by holding onto a "thread tail." Pull taut as you begin to stitch.

"thread tail"

• Use tear-away non-wovens at the beginning of seams. Overlap the fashion fabric and the tear-away. Start stitching on the tear-away, then right onto the fabric. Tear-away the non-woven after stitching.

tear-away non-woven

silky fabric

• It's best not to backstitch at the very beginning and end of seams . . . jamming can easily occur. That's usually not where you need the reinforcement anyway. Instead, at seam intersection points (⅝" into the seam or the seam width) move the stitch length to a tiny 15-18 stitches per inch or backstitch.

tiny stitches or backstitch ⅝" into seam

• Try "taut sewing" — it helps prevent puckering and skipped stitches. This method is borrowed from my publisher's best-selling book, **Mother Pletsch's Painless Sewing**. Pull equally on your fabric in front of and behind the needle as you sew. Do not stretch, just pull taut as if you were sewing with your fabric in an embroidery hoop. However, let the fabric feed through the machine on its own.

"taut sewing"

pull equally

• "Continuous sewing," can also help prevent jamming at the beginning of seams.

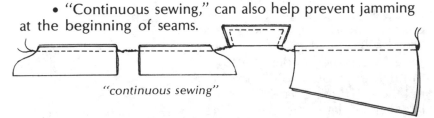

"continuous sewing"

PROBLEM: "Puckery" seams and edges.

SOLUTIONS:

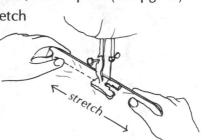

- Use taut sewing (see pg. 54).

- "Seal the seam" — press flat, then open. (see pg. 69).

- On knits like Qiana®, stretch the seam slightly while sewing. Then seal the seam.

NOTE: Often puckers occur at the bottom of a knit skirt seam . . . the weight of the knit causes it to hang out more than the thread will give. Stretch to the full extent at the bottom as you approach the hem edge.

- Change to a new, smaller machine needle size (see pg. 45) and finer thread (see pg. 43).

- If possible, adjust the "pressure regulator," which changes the amount of pressure on the foot. When the pressure is correct, the fabric is held firmly but not too tightly in place. Because of the light weight of silkies, you may need more foot pressure. See your sewing machine manual.

- On some machines there is no pressure regulator — then work on stitch tension.

- On very lightweight silkies and sheers, try placing tissue paper (or any paper that's handy like adding machine tape, typing paper, etc.) under the seams next to the feed dog — on top of the seams too, if necessary. Pull away the paper after the seam is sewn.

- Staystitching can tighten edges unnecessarily on light weight silks and silkies. Staystitch only neckline areas.

- Try sewing with a shorter stitch — 12-15 stitches/inch. The lighter weight silkies seem to pucker less with a shorter stitch. Smaller stitches use more thread and puckers are caused by too little thread and tight tension.

• Adjust the machine tension — it may be too tight or improperly balanced. Remember, turn RIGHT TO TIGHTEN, LEFT TO LOOSEN. As a last resort, adjust the bobbin screw or dial. See your machine manual.

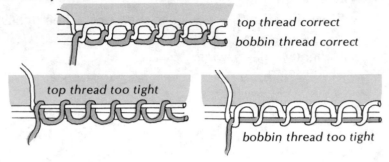

top thread correct
bobbin thread correct

top thread too tight

bobbin thread too tight

• Change the needle and thread size, usually to smaller and finer.

• Wind your bobbin thread slowly. When synthetic threads, like polyester types, are wound too fast it causes stretching of the thread. The seams then pucker when the thread relaxes.

PROBLEM: "Skipped machine stitches" the top thread doesn't form a loop with the bobbin thread.

SOLUTIONS:
• Try prewashing your fabric. Finishes, both synthetic (on polyesters, nylons, rayons, triacetates, etc.) and natural (on silks), can gum up your machine needle and cause skipped stitches.

• Stitch more slowly, at an even pace. Some machines have a slower, low gear.

• Change needles. Damaged needles are candidates for the garbage can! Singer® Yellow Band (for knits) and Red Band (for wovens) have a longer scarf (needle indentation) so they pick up the bobbin thread more easily. Experiment with different needle sizes.

• Change thread. Try another type, brand and/or size. It's easier to balance your stitch if the same thread is used on the top and bobbin.

• Convert to a small hole needle plate or fill in with tape (see pg. 53).

• I've tried many different sewing machines and, on

some, skipped stitches are a real problem. If you're buying a machine take several "skip-prone" samples for test stitching — like silkies, knits, synthetic suede, etc. Starched cotton batiste doesn't prove anything!

• Sew with a very, very slight zigzag on knits.

PROBLEM: The thread keeps breaking or stripping back.
SOLUTIONS:
• Change needle. It may be damaged, have a burr in the eye or be too small for the thread.

• Test different thread types. I was trying to zigzag with some old cotton thread (could have been 15 years old!) and it kept breaking. Was something wrong with my machine? NO. I changed to newer synthetic thread — no more breaking!

• Check your threading. If it's incorrect the thread will break.

PROBLEM: The top layer of fabric is scooting forward, making seam layers uneven.
SOLUTIONS:
• Try a roller foot or even feed type of foot.

• Marjorie Arch (of the famous Bishop Method) taught Pati Palmer a neat trick to help solve this problem. Lift the presser foot very slightly — it's amazing how the top layer will feed right in. Don't really raise the foot . . . just lighten as you sew.

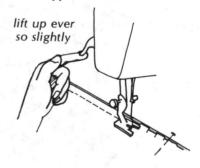
lift up ever so slightly

• Lighten machine pressure on presser foot.

PROBLEM: The seam is wrong — you need to rip it out.
SOLUTIONS:
• Cut stitches with seam ripper every inch on one side of seam. Pull thread on other side. Brush off or pull out small clipped threads. Sometimes steaming will remove needle holes.

CHAPTER NINE

Seam Finishes

Some seamsters mistakenly assume that if they pay more for a fabric, they should "pray" more (in other words, spend lots of time on finishing details). Not so, "less is better" on silkies. Zigzagging, taping or putting lace on seams can show through to the right side.

TEST seam finishes on your fabric swatches. Wider seams (1"+) are the easiest to finish.

Seam Finishing Methods

- The easiest finish for conventional seams is just **straight stitching** ¼" from the raw edges and pinking. (Straight stitching the seam edges may even show through to the right side on some silkies — in that case, pink only.)

- You can finish with **Fray-check**™ — use it sparingly on silkies!

- Edges can be "**serpentine**" stitched (3 step zigzag) — it bunches up the fabric less than regular zigzagging.

- Raw edges can also be **hand overcast** — but yee gads — who has time?

- Bias seams need no finish since bias will not ravel.

 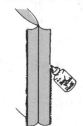 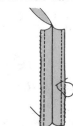

pinked (with or without machine stitching) NOTE: Pink both edges together to save time if possible.

Fray-Check™ *(without stitching for the least bulk)*

serpentine stitch (use taut sewing so it will lie flat.)

hand overcast (with or without machine stitching)

NOTE: The less the garment is worn and laundered, the less seam finishing or special seaming is necessary. On a silk camisole that I made for evening wear, the seams were just pinked. Yet on a polyester georgette blouse for everyday wear I used French seams.

Turned and Stitched Seam Finishes

Uses: Lightweight silkies, straight seams.

CAUTION: This will create some bulk on the seam edge. DO NOT press over the seam edges — seam indentations will show on the right side.

Allow 1" seam allowances. Stitch along the seamline. "Seal the seam" (see pg. 69). Turn under the seam allowances ¼" and straight stitch ⅛" from the fold. Stitch from the right side as shown to control slippery raw edges better.

The Easy Narrow Seam Finish

Uses: For sheers or any lightweight silky fabric including ravel-prone types. Any straight or curved seam.

Straight stitch along the seamline. Stitch again, ¼" from the first stitching into the seam allowance (or use a medium zigzag or blind hemstitch). Trim close to this stitching. Press seam allowances toward the back of the garment.

¼" straight stitch

¼" zig-zag

¼" blind hemstitch

NOTE: Another neat, new seam finish (not shown) is over-edging done with a serger, now readily available to home seamsters.

"Seams Great"™ or "Seams Saver"™ Seam Finish

Uses: Sheers or any light to medium weight silky fabric. Straight or curved seams. TEST FIRST!

Stitch along the seamline. Trim the seam allowances to ¼". Enclose the seam allowances in ⅝" Seams Great or Seams Saver. (These are precut strips of nylon tricot knit that won't ravel.) The strip automatically folds in one direction only. Pull to see which direction before stitching over seam. Only one row of stitching is needed to apply — pull the tricot strip slightly taut while stitching so it will wrap over seam allowances as shown. Test iron temperature on the nylon before pressing the seams.

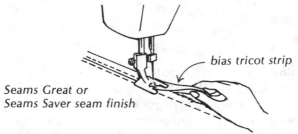

bias tricot strip

Seams Great or
Seams Saver seam finish

Traditional Oriental Silk Seam Finishes

Turned and Handstitched
Uses: Medium to heavy weight silks, especially brocade and textured types. Straight or curved edges. Perfect for quilted coats and vests, and lighter weight kimonos.

Stitch along the seamline. Press flat and then open or to the back of the garment. Hand blindstitch the edges under and to the garment. The stitching slightly shows on the right side, but that's part of the look.

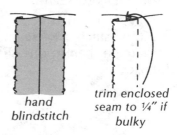

hand
blindstitch

trim enclosed
seam to ¼" if
bulky

The Hong Kong Seam Finish
Uses: For straight or curved seams in medium to heavier weight fabrics. You'll love it for unlined jackets — be a little jazzy and use a print for the bias strips!

Cut 1" wide bias strips (see pg. 80) out of lining or underlining fabric. (For lots and lots of seams consider using our continuous bias method, pg. 81). Sew the bias strip to the seam edge, right sides together, with a ¼" seam allowance. Try not to stretch the bias as you stitch — this can prevent the seam from lying flat. Wrap the seam raw edge with the bias strip. From the right side, stitch in the ditch. You're done! Gorgeous.

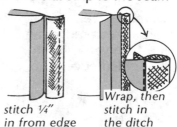

stitch ¼"
in from edge

Wrap, then
stitch in
the ditch

CHAPTER TEN

Special Seams

Sometimes a special seam, rather than just a finish is required to prevent raveling for a neater, narrower look on sheers, or occasionally for durability. Test on your fabric before seaming your garment — most are a mess to rip out!

The French Seam

Uses: I reserve this seam for sheers and ravel-prone fabrics that will be laundered a lot. This is a narrow, delicate seam that is only 2 rows of stitching. It's actually faster than stitching some seam finishes. It's easiest on straight or only slightly curved seams.

With wrong sides together, stitch a ⅜" seam. Press open then to one side. Trim to ⅛".

Fold right sides together. Stitch a seam ¼" from the fold. Press the seam allowances toward the back of the garment.

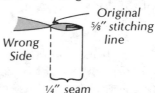

The Mock French Seam

Uses: This "French" seam can be used for just about any seam, even armholes. However, straight or only slightly curved seams are easiest.

Stitch along the seamline. Press open. Fold in seam edges and topstitch very close to the folded edges.

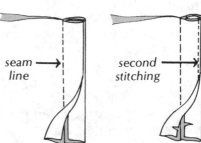

Wrapped Seam

Uses: Sheers to medium weight silkies. Straight or slightly curved seams.

Allow 1" seams when cutting for easier handling. Stitch along the seamline. Press the seam open. Trim the seam allowance to the back of the garment to ¼".

Fold under the raw edge of wider seam allowance about ¼".

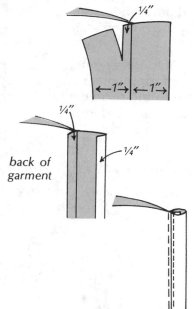

back of garment

Bring wider seam allowance over the trimmed layer.

Stitch along the fold as close to the first seam stitching line as possible.

Variation: In case you didn't cut wider seams, for standard ⅝" seams, trim one side to ⅛" and wrap the other side over. The seam will be narrow and a bit more difficult to handle — but will look "rolled."

Topstitched Seam

Uses: Light to heavyweight silks. Straight or curved seams. This method makes very durable, ravel-resistant seams.

Straight stitch along the seam line. Press the seam open. Now press both seam allowances toward the back of the garment. Clip into the curved seams before topstitching if necessary to lie flat. Topstitch from the right side about ⅜" from the seamline. Trim to the stitching line.

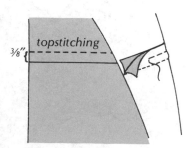

topstitching

Variations:
For a more padded look, or on medium to heavy knits, trim the hidden seam to ¼".

Or add another row of topstitching close to the seamline to give a flat-felled look.

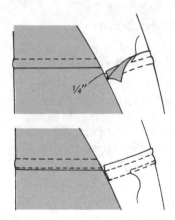

Enclosed Swiss Edge for Sheer Fabrics

Uses: Collars, cuffs, etc. Prevents ravelly, uneven seam from showing through.

Place right sides together. Stitch a Swiss Edge hem finish (see Chapter 23, pg. 125) along the seam line. Trim to the stitching. Turn right sides out.

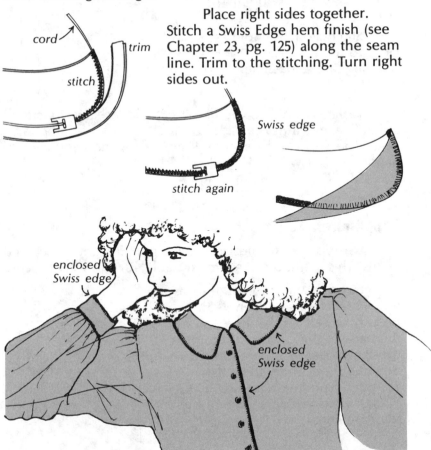

CHAPTER ELEVEN
Darts, Ease and Gathers

Convert Darts to Easing

Whenever possible, I eliminate darts in lightweight silky garments. I prefer soft easing, especially replacing vertical darts. Some double pointed vertical darts can be eliminated altogether — wear the garment loose or belted.

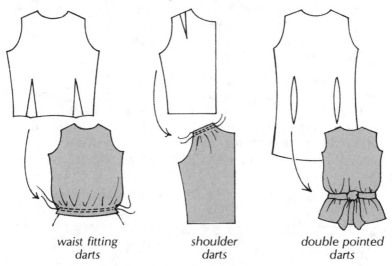

| waist fitting darts | shoulder darts | double pointed darts |

How to Ease Rather Than Dart

Mark the dart stitching lines on your fabric with snips. Start and stop ease stitching lines about ½″ on either side of the dart stitching lines (snips).

Stitch two rows of baste stitching, one at ⅜″ and at ⅝″. Pull up top or bottom threads until the dart fullness has been taken up.

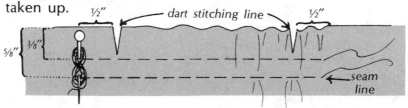

Stitching Darts in Silkies

Start stitching toward the point, shortening the stitch length to 15/inch for the last ½-1". Do not backstitch at the point — let your machine "chain off." Cut the threads leaving a long tail. **OR** pull dart toward you with needle up and machine stitch the chain into dart seam allowance.

Start stitching in the center of double pointed darts and stitch out to each point. That way it's easier to get fine, pucker-free points.

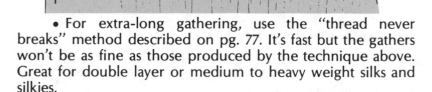

Gathering Tips

• For very fine gathers, stitch ⅜" and ⅝" from the edge using about 8-9 stitches per inch rather than a basting length. Secure the top or bottom threads at one end by wrapping around a pin and draw up the other. Use heavier thread like buttonhole twist on the top or bobbin to prevent thread breakage. When seaming, stitch just outside the ⅝" basting line.

• For extra-long gathering, use the "thread never breaks" method described on pg. 77. It's fast but the gathers won't be as fine as those produced by the technique above. Great for double layer or medium to heavy weight silks and silkies.

• Distribute the gathers evenly (see pg. 77).

• To keep the gathers even while stitching in place, hold them taut between your forefingers, perpendicular to the seamline. Stitch just outside the ⅝" line, then remove ⅝" basting.

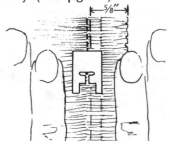

CHAPTER TWELVE
Pressing as You Sew

Since my days in the bridal dressmaking department I've realized how important proper pressing is. Lightweight silkies, especially synthetics, can be **over pressed** and **over handled**.

And need we remind you? Yes, always *TEST*. Various silky fabrics respond differently to heat and steam.

Your Iron

The Sunbeam "Shot-of-Steam®" and the lightweight G. E. "Surge of Steam®" are favorites of mine. The extra jet of steam makes seams press flatter and fusing faster.

press cloth

If you've got an iron that spits, and water spots and/or steams poorly, junk it. Experience sewing success with a new iron.

The Right Tools Help

• To press cloth or not to press cloth . . . it's a must on the right side of some delicate surface synthetics, and when fusing! Many synthetics require both construction pressing and top pressing with a press cloth for a crisp seam or edge.

• Iron sole plates like Iron Safe® and Iron All® make old irons like new and protect fabric surfaces, minimizing shine, without a press cloth. These covers buffer the temperature lowering it slightly, so a higher setting may be necessary.

soleplate cover

• If you haven't covered the iron with a sole plate, clean it frequently with a hot iron cleaner like Clean and Glide™ (Stacy) or Iron Off™ (Dritz). They easily remove fusible residue as well as cleaning.

• Replace those shiny silicone ironing board covers —
they can make the fabric too hot and even can cause synthetics to melt. These covers bounce steam and heat back into the
fabric and cause overheating. Instead, pad the ironing board
with an absorbent old wool blanket. Buy an all cotton board
cover like that available through the June Tailor Company or
cover with gingham or muslin using the old cover as a pattern.

Test the Temperature

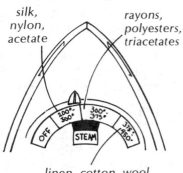

silk, nylon, acetate

rayons, polyesters, triacetates

linen, cotton, wool

• Set your iron on the
correct temperature. The setting
for real silk should be a low steam
setting (275°-300° F).

• *Always* test
when it comes to
deciding on steam
or dry heat. Most
synthetics require
steam to minimize shine
. . . some silks should be pressed
dry. I prefer steam for most!

• Always let the fabric cool before moving. Fabrics have
a memory only when cool.

• What to do about "glazing" (an undesirable shine on
the fabric surface due to excessive and/or too dry heat). It
shows most on dark and intense colors.
   — On silks and rayons: For small area, use a 2:1 vinegar/
      water solution on the press cloth. Colors may run
      on high contrast prints or intense shades. Test first in
      an inconspicuous area. Washing the entire garment
      may also remove the shiny area.
   — On silky synthetics like polyesters, nylons, triacetates
      and acetates, glazing can be permanent as you've
      melted the surface fibers. Use a cooler iron and/or a
      press cloth next time!!

Where Not to Press:
   • The right side without testing first
   • Over pins
   • Sleeve caps (see pg. 103)
   • Over hem or facing edges.

Pressing How-to's

- Check the garment fit *before* pressing seams and darts.

"Seal the seam" first, by pressing it as shown, then open.

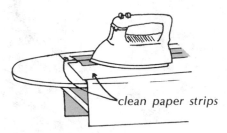

Use a light hand press — not too much pressure. A gentle up and down motion is best.

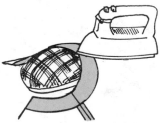

seam roll

Prevent seam imprint by pressing over a seam roll.

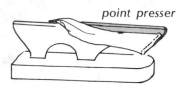

clean paper strips

Place strips of paper under edges of seams if you have no seam roll.

Press darts, curved seams and facings over a pressing ham.

point presser

Use a combination point presser/clapper for pressing open enclosed seams before they are turned. (Such as collar seams.)

clapper

Use a clapper to hold in iron steam and heat without overpressing.

CHAPTER THIRTEEN

Tucks, Pleats and Ruffles

These "easy extras" are perfect for silk and silkies. Many mistakenly assume that these details are difficult and time consuming, but with these tips they needn't be. Notice how much variety can be added to the simplest of styles at collars, cuffs, bodices, hems.

Easy, Even Tucks

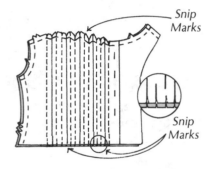

Snip Marks

Snip Marks

1. Mark by the "snip mark, and press" method. Snip mark the tuck fold and stitching line at the top and bottom edges. On long tucks you may need to pin mark the fold halfway. Washable marker can help mark too, but test first for removability.

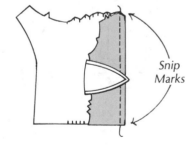

Snip Marks

2. Take the fabric piece to your ironing board. Press along the foldline of the outermost tuck (it's easier than working from the center). Press and stitch only one tuck at a time . . . honestly, it's faster and more accurate.

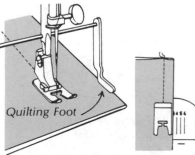

3. Use your presser foot, quilting foot, magnetic seam guide, or masking tape on the throat plate to keep the stitching even the entire length of the tuck. Use taut sewing (see pg. 54) to prevent puckering.

Quilting Foot

4. Go back to the ironing board and press the next tuck fold line. Stitch as instructed in Step 3.

5. Press each tuck after it is stitched to check width evenness ˉand spacing. Then press all tucks in one direction or toward sides of garment. Use a press cloth when pressing on the right side.

6. Staystitch across the ends of tucks to hold them in position.

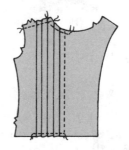

Add Tucks to Any Pattern

The easiest way is to tuck the fabric *before* you cut the garment.

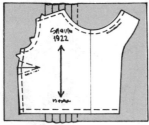

If you need to piece your fabric because you run out of length or width, piece along a stitching line and it will be hidden by the tuck.

Types of Tucks

Blind tucks — no spaces between tucks. Great for silks. Adds body and a degree of modesty.

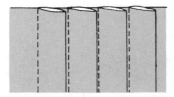

Spaced tucks — uses less fabric than blind tucks.

Varied Width Tucks
Start with narrow tucks ⅛" deep and gradually widen the tucks.

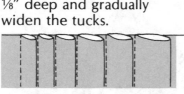

NOTE: The spacing between the tuck stitching should be increased as the tucks get larger. Increase the spacing by ½ the total increase in the tuck.

Cross Tucking
Stitch spaced tucks and press in one direction first then stitch tucks in the opposite direction. Great for detail areas!

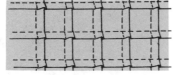

Twisted Tucking
Stitch spaced tucks then topstitch alternately the direction of the tuck.

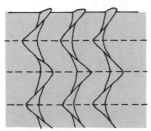

NOTE: The tucks shouldn't be wider than ½" or the topstitching will cause pulling.

Pin Tucks

• Plain pin tucks are just narrow tucks.

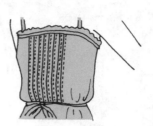

• Pin tucks can be created by using a double needle (a special foot helps keep rows even). The common bobbin thread draws up the two top threads creating a tuck. Consult your machine manual.

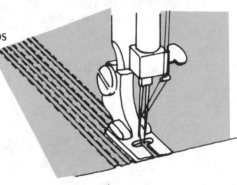

• For a rounder, wider, pin tuck, use zipper foot as shown. Sportweight yarn or preshrunk cotton string works well as filler.

• For picot edge pin tucks, set your machine on a blind hemstitch. The zigzag stitch will pull in the edge fold creating a picot edge.

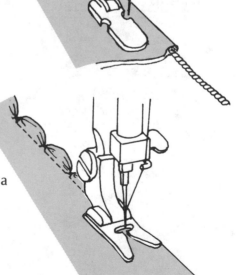

Easy, Even Pleats

Use the "snip mark and press" method used for tucks (see pg. 71). Pin, hand or machine baste pleats closed during pressing and fitting (If you fit a garment too tight, the pleats won't lie flat.).

Pressing Pleats

Strips of paper (typing or tissue) will cushion the edges so a ridge won't form on the under layers.

press cloth

paper
strips

Adding Pleats

A single inverted pleat (or box pleat) is easily added to the center back or front of a garment by placing the center back 1-2" from the fold.

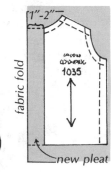

1"-2"

fabric fold

1035

new pleat

Pleats in a Striped Fabric

On a recent visit to Richard Brooks Fabrics in Dallas, we saw a two piece blouse and skirt made by department manager, Sandy Sandstrom. She used a 5-color silk stripe. The black, royal blue and white stripes showed. The fuschia and emerald were pleated out and only showed with movement. Fabulous! Here's a few tips from Sandy:

- Pre-pleat the fabric. Press along silk stripe line and edge stitch to keep pleats flat. Piece fabric under a pleat if necessary (shown in tucks, pg. 72). Baste pleats closed.

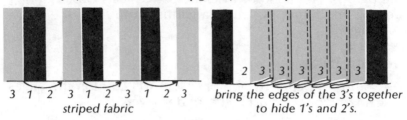

3 1 2 3 1 2 3 1 2 3
striped fabric

2 3 3 3 3 3 3
bring the edges of the 3's together to hide 1's and 2's.

- Edgestitch to hold pleat edges. It's easiest to hem edges first before edgestitching or cutting the pieces out — plan layout accordingly.

- Cut out pattern over pre-pleated fabric.

- Topstitch areas you don't want to release like a waistline, cuff or hipline.

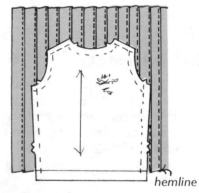

hemline

right side

Machine made Pleats

Most machine rufflers can be adjusted to pleat. I've found these machine-made pleats (often called plaiting) perfect for pleated trim. Follow attachment instructions and experiment with ruffler gauges, stitch length and tension. Run a test sample to determine the amount of "take-up". Cut fabric strips accordingly allowing extra length for goof-proofing.

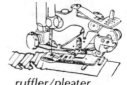

ruffler/pleater

Soft Ruffles

Cutting

Cut the ruffle length at least twice as long as the edge or area to be trimmed . . . up to three times as long for lighter weight sheers. Skimpy ruffles look too flat.

The grain can be lengthwise, crosswise or bias. For straight grains, piece straight. For softer bias ruffles, piece on the diagonal (see Chapter 14, pg. 80). For long distance ruffles, use the continuous bias strip method (pg. 81).

Gathering

• To gather the strips, I prefer the "thread never breaks" method. Just inside the seam line zigzag with a medium width, long stitch over but not catching a heavier thread. The shorter you gauge the stitch, the finer the gathers will be. Secure one end of the heavier thread by wrapping it in a figure eight over a large head pin. Draw up the heavier thread — no more broken basting stitches — yeah! Also see pg. 66.

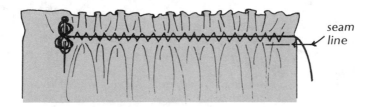

seam line

• Divide the ruffle strips and garment into quarters by marking with pins or snips before sewing on the ruffle, to make sure the gathers will be distributed evenly.

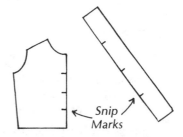

Snip Marks

When arranging gathers allow more gathers on outside curves and corners, less on inside curves and corners. The gathers will look like they are distributed evenly.

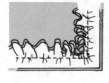 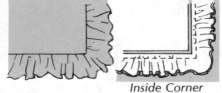

Outside Corner   Inside Corner

• Have you tried your machine's gathering foot? Refer to your machine manual . . . generally the tighter the tension and the longer the stitch, the more it gathers. Do a test run first to determine how much "take up" there will be in the gathering.

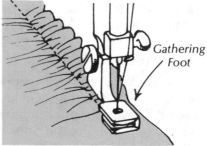

Gathering Foot

• Use narrow hems on ruffles. (See Chpt. 22, pg. 121-126).

• Finish ruffle ends by:

tapering into seamline,

turning raw edges under twice and stitching by hand or machine

or, on double layer ruffles, turning ends in and hand blindstitching.

Pressing Ruffles

Generally press the seam allowances together, not open.

Seams pressed in the same direction as the ruffle will stand up more . . . in the opposite direction will lie flatter (seam allowances can be topstitched in place).

Press the ruffle and garment separately to avoid flattening the ruffle.

CHAPTER FOURTEEN
On the Bias

What is bias?

Bias is a diagonal line halfway between the lengthwise and crosswise grain on the fabric, creating a grainline that gives.

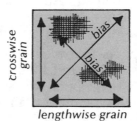

lengthwise grain

Cutting a Garment on the Bias.

Even if your pattern doesn't specify bias grain, you can cut it on the bias. Why?

- Bias drapes beautifully
- Bias will be more comfortable to wear in fitted areas like sleeves.
- Bias is ravel-free on seam and hem edges — no finishing!

How to Change a Pattern to a Bias Cut

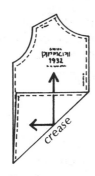

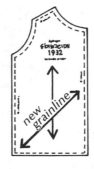

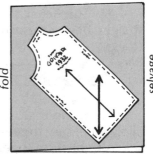

- *Fold tissue so that the grainline is at a 90° angle to itself.*

- *The crease will be the new grainline.*

- *Lay the new grainline on the length or crosswise grain of the fabric.*

Bias Sewing Tips

• Cut 2" side seam allowances for fitting insurance — you will need it! Bias pieces narrow as they hang.

• Hang pieces 24 hours before seaming.

• Bias cut garments shouldn't be too tight-fitting as seams will ripple.

• Stretch seams as you sew. Because the bias stretches more than your thread, it can cause pulling and puckering along seamlines. You may also try a very narrow zigzag for more built-in "give" in seams.

• Zippers are easier to put in the center back seams than side seams. Avoid stretching the bias fabric when stitching the zipper in. (The zipper will also buckle if skirt is too tight.) Actually, I prefer pull-on and wrap styles for bias, avoiding zippers altogether.

• Measure hem from the floor up using a yardstick as the bias will hang out unevenly.

• Narrow machine hems are nice on bias garments and edges. Stretch slightly as you sew to get a ruffled effect.

Cutting Bias Strips

Uses: tubing, (pg. 81), binding and spaghetti straps (see pgs. 83-85), piping (pg. 87).

1. Fold fabric so lengthwise and crosswise grains are parallel. Mark width of strips and cut.

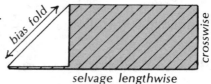

selvage lengthwise

2. The seam that joins the bias strips must be on the straight of grain (seam will be diagonal). If you piece with a straight seam it will stretch because the seamline will be on the bias.

3. Using a ¼" seam allowance, sew the piecing seams right sides together. Line the strips together at the ¼" seam lines, not at the end edges.

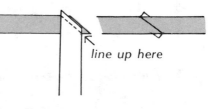

line up here

Continuous Bias Already Pieced!

Use this easy bias strip method whenever you need long strips for bindings, pipings or facings. The width of any binding technique can be varied. Experiment after mastering the basics.

1. Using a 2" wide cardboard or ruler template, mark the 2" wide bias strips on the fabric with washable marking pen or tailor's chalk pencil. Cut the fabric where shown.

2. Seam the selvage edges, staggering the ends so that the bias strip can be cut continuously. Press open the seam.

(illus)

3. Cut along the marked lines.

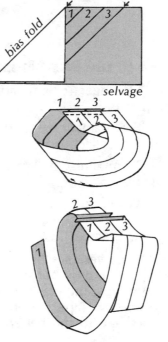

Easy Bias Tubing

Uses: belts, drawstrings, ties and spaghetti straps

Fabrics: Just about any fabric, but sheer to medium weights are best for very narrow tubes.

1. Cut the bias strips 4-5 times wider than the finished width (5-6 times wider for sheers). The lighter weight the fabric the wider the seam allowance (the seam allowance is not trimmed but fills the tube).

2. Stitch right sides together. The seam allowance should be equal to or wider than half the finished tube width. Stitch with a narrower seam allowance at the end for easier turning.

3. Turn the tube right sides out. Try any one of these turning tools. Push the fabric over the tool until the fabric is right side out.

ballpoint bodkin   *bobby pin*   *pencil eraser*

CHAPTER FIFTEEN

Bias Bindings

Where to use Bias Bindings:

• On sheers or any fabric transparent enough to show facings.

• For dramatic effect or accents; contrasting colors and texture on collars, lapels, cuffs, necklines, hems.

• To minimize bulk on heavier fabrics, simply use lighter weight bias bindings.

• When you don't have enough self-fabric for facings!

Shaping Bias

On curves bias bindings may need to be pre-shaped. Steam press, but do not stretch excessively. Too much stretching will narrow the bias strip and take out all the natural give and resiliency. Tape pattern pieces together. Press the bias strip to shape to the pattern curve.

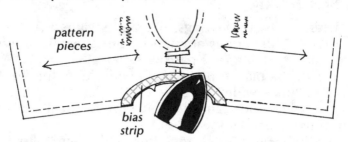

pattern pieces

bias strip

When shaping strips for French binding, fold in half first, wrong sides together, then press.

When pinning to garment, stretch bias strip slightly on inward curves, ease bias strip slightly on outward curves.

stretch and press

ease press

French Binding

Use this method for sheer to lightweight fabrics. The binding is sewn on double layer for a soft, rounded effect. Since it is finished with handstitching, it is well-suited for sheer and lightweight silkies.

1. Cut 2" wide bias strips . . . for long strips, see the Continuous Bias Method, pg. 81. Fold the strip in half lengthwise. Press and shape the binding if necessary.

2. Trim off the garment seam or hem allowance completely.

3. Pin the binding to the edge right sides together, keeping the raw edges even. Stitch a ¼" seam allowance.

4. Turn the binding over the seam allowances and hand blindstitch in place.

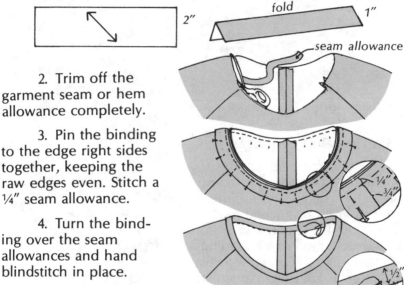

Fast French Binding

Use this method for light to heavier weight fabrics. The binding is sewn on single layer so it is less rounded than French binding, but it is done entirely by machine so it's really fast!

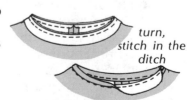

turn, stitch in the ditch

Trim off the garment seam or hem allowance. Apply the bias strip to the edge, single layer. Turn the binding to the garment wrong side encasing the raw edge. From the garment right side, stitch in the ditch or seam "groove" to hold the binding in place.

Joining Bias Bindings

Start stitching at an inconspicuous point. Trim the strip end off straight, not at an angle. Fold the binding end to the wrong side ½" or so. Align the fold with the seam line. To finish, extend the binding over the folded edge, staggering the layers to minimize bulk. Fold the binding to the wrong side and secure with machine or hand stitching. This seam should not be stitched — it will "give" better. If stitched it could pucker.

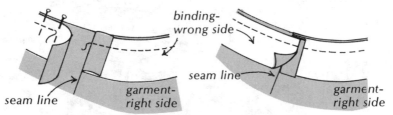

binding-
wrong side

seam line

garment-
right side

seam line

seam line

garment-
right side

Mitering Bias Bindings

These mitered corners are guaranteed beginner-proof and perfect for silkies because they are soft and not stitched to a point. Use these corners for both French and fast French bindings. If you've never worked with bias bindings or are using particularly slippery fabric, test first on a scrap.

Outward Corners

1. Right sides together, stitch the bias strip to the exact corner point. Shorten stitches (15-20/inch) upon approaching the point. Backstitch a couple of stitches.

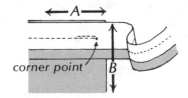

←—A—→

corner point

B

2. Now fold the strip so the folded edge is even with the "A" edge. Press lightly with iron to hold in place.

3. Stitch from the "A" edge along the "B" edge, using the exact seam allowance (any variance will make a messy miter).

4. Turn the binding to fold over the edge. Work toward the corner from both sides pinning the binding to the finished width. Form a miter at the corner . . . the miter will almost fall into place.

5. To finish the wrong side, form a miter with a fold in the opposite direction to minimize bulk. Pin or tape in place. Hand blind-stitch or machine stitch in the ditch.

Inward Corner

1. Reinforce the corner along the seamline with a very short (18-20/inch) stitch. Clip right to the corner point.

2. Straighten corner and pin strip to the edge.

3. Stitch the binding to the edge from the garment side to make sure you stitch beyond the clip.

4. Working toward the corner from both directions, pin the binding keeping width even. Form a miter on the right side.

5. Pull the miter fold through the corner clip. Form another miter on the wrong side. To minimize bulk, reverse miter direction on the other side. Secure with tape or pins and machine or hand stitch in place.

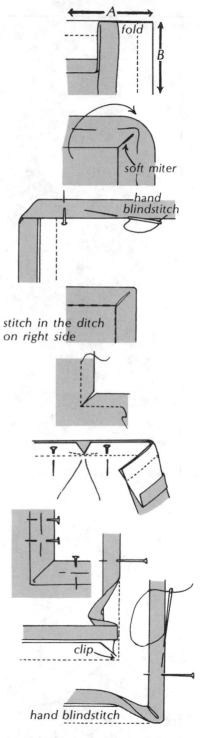

soft miter

hand blindstitch

stitch in the ditch on right side

clip

hand blindstitch

CHAPTER SIXTEEN

𝒫erfect 𝒫iping

Piping Uses

- As a decorative finish in any seam (strengthens seams as well).

- As an edge trim with facings.

- As an edge finish period, without facings.

Buying Piping

Look for satin piping, decorative braids, loop braids, and cords that have one flat edge. Preshrink if washable before using, even if the garment is to be dry cleaned. Soak in hot water 10 minutes, line dry.

Making Piping

1. Cut bias strips 1½" wide (see pg. 81 for continuous bias) — just the right finished width for ⅝" seams. The strips must be cut on the *true* bias (see pg. 79) for twist-free piping.

2. Fold the bias over yarn, wrong sides together. Strands of acrylic sportweight (fine) yarn work well because they remain flexible and don't shrink. Experiment with other piping fillers like pre-shrunk crochet cotton, cotton string, cable cord, or very tiny cotton cording.

3. Put the zipper foot on your machine and set the stitch length to 10/inch. Stitch across the strip ½" from the piping end, securing the filler in place.

zipper foot

½"

4. Stitch close to the filler. The bias strip will stretch slightly when stitching but avoid excessive stretching.

5. For more than one length of piping, don't stop stitching between strips.

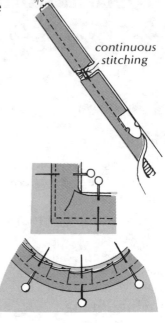

continuous stitching

Attaching Piping to Garment

1. Place the piping stitching line directly over the garment seam or hemline. Clip and notch into the piping where needed.

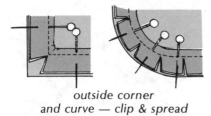

outside corner
and curve — clip & spread

inside corner
and curve — notch & lap

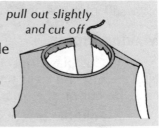

NOTE: On an inside curve, like a neck edge, you may find it helpful to pull up the cording inside the piping to pull in the edge slightly and reduce bulk. Pull up to desired length and secure with stitching. Cut off the excess end.

pull out slightly and cut off

2. Stitch directly on top of the stitching line that formed the piping.

Finishing

1. Pin the facing, lining or corresponding seam to the piped edge.

2. Always stitch from the side that has been piped so that you can stitch directly over that line of stitching for even piping everytime.

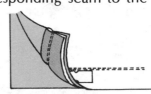

3. Press the seam open. Then seam edges should be pressed opposite the piping direction as shown. Topstitching is optional.

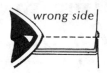

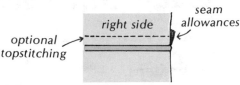

Piping As An Edge Finish

If the piping is the edge finish without a facing, simply turn the piping edges to the wrong side. Trim, grade and understitch as necessary. Press very lightly. You may also want to edgestitch or topstitch the piping in place.

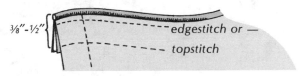

Joining Piping

Start stitching at an inconspicuous point, angling the piping into the seam allowance. To finish, overlap the piping and angle into the seam allowance — you may need to remove some of the filler to minimize bulk.

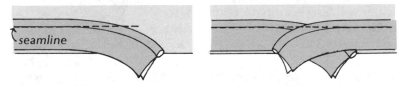

To Start and Finish Piping At An Edge

Rip out some of the first piping stitching. Fold the piping edge to the wrong side.

Trim the filler to the edge. Finish the piping end with handstitching.

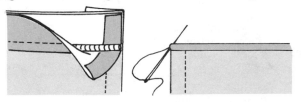

CHAPTER SEVENTEEN

Fool-proof Facings and Edge Finishes

The Easy Steps

Staystitch

Directionally staystitch curved edges like necklines to prevent stretching. Fit before finishing edges.

Interface

Using a fusible on the facing rather than on the garment is one of the quickest, most foolproof ways to stabilize and finish an edge. The fusible will also eliminate raveling, so no facing edge finish is needed. Also see Chapter 5.

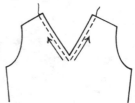

right side

fusible interfacing

NOTE: if your facing stretches out slightly before you fuse to it, steam "ease" back into shape before fusing, using pattern piece as a guide for size.

You may want to stitch ¼" from the edge and pink on more ravel prone fabrics.

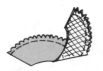

stitch and pink

Occasionally on very lightweight fabrics, the stitch line can "press through" or pucker — then pinking only is best.

pink

Stitch and Trim

- **Stitch facing seams** with a short stitch at least 15 stitches/inch, at curves and corners (anywhere clipping is necessary). This prevents ripping or raveling out.

Curves
like armholes

Inside corner
like square
neckline

Outside corner
like cuff

"V" Necklines

- For medium and heavyweight silks and silkies, **grade enclosed seams by beveling.** Slant shears until they are almost flat over the seam. On lighter weight silks and silkies, grading is often unnecessary.

- **Notch outward curves** with pinking shears.

- **For inward curves alternate clipping** on the facing and garment layers to prevent rippling on the right side and strengthen the seam.

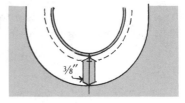

outward curve

inward curve

- To **minimize bulk,** trim facing seam allowances to ⅜″ and angle intersecting seams.

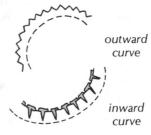

⅜″

Hiding Facings — Two Methods

1. **Understitch.** Stitch facing and seam allowances together close to the seam from the facing side. Always clip and trim **before** understitching.

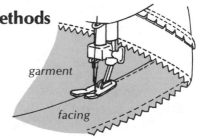

garment

facing

OR 2. Roll the seams to the inside and press the edge.

Optional: Press carefully on the right side over a ham, using a see-through press cloth.

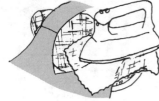

Keep Facings Flat — Two Methods

1. Lightly hand tack down facings to shoulders, underarms, side seams, etc.

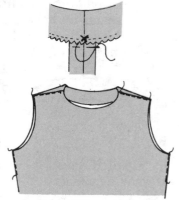

OR 2. Stitch in the ditch — directly in the seam indentation from the right side. Shorter stitches (12-15/inch) will be more easily hidden in lightweight silks and silkies.

The Perfect Fit "V" Neckline — Good-bye Gaposis

The "V" neckline is one of the most flattering. The lines draw attention to the face, de-emphasize the hips and create the illusion of height. But when the bias edges stretch and gap out away from our chests — you get "V" neckline gaposis!

1. Try on the tissue paper pattern to check the "V" depth.

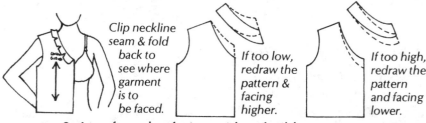

Clip neckline seam & fold back to see where garment is to be faced.

If too low, redraw the pattern & facing higher.

If too high, redraw the pattern and facing lower.

2. Interface the facing with a fusible non-woven interfacing to stabilize the "V". Remember to "steam ease" the facing to the pattern if the facing has stretched (pg. 90).

3. Place woven edge seam binding (pre-shrink before using) on the wrong side to stabilize the "V". Pull tape shorter so neckline will hug chest.

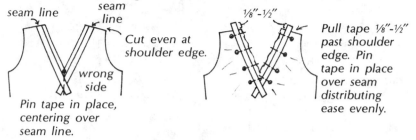

seam line

seam line

Cut even at shoulder edge.

wrong side

Pin tape in place, centering over seam line.

⅛"-½"

Pull tape ⅛"-½" past shoulder edge. Pin tape in place over seam distributing ease evenly.

4. Check fit by pinning the front to the back and trying it on.

5. Stitch tape to "V". Sew directionally from the point to each shoulder. Stitch through the center of the tape with the tape side on top. The feed dog on your machine will ease the fabric into the tape.

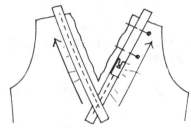

6. Stitch garment shoulder seams.

7. Apply facings by matching first to center front and center back of garment. If you shortened the neckline tape, the front facing will be larger than neckline. Adjust the facing at the shoulder seam.

8. Proceed as previously described for other facings. The "V" neckline should fit better than ever no matter what fabric you're using!

Facing Options for Silks and Silkies

Faced Facing

This technique interfaces the edge and finishes the facing all-in-one. It can be used for both cut-on and sewn-on facings. The facing edge will be slightly bulkier than conventional facings.

1. Use silk or synthetic organza, self-fabric (if very lightweight), PolySiBonne Plus, or fusible interfacing like Easy Knit, Sheer Weight Fusible Pellon or SoSheer by Armo.

2. Using a ¼" seam, stitch the interfacing to the outer edge of the facing, right sides together. Use a short stitch (15/inch or so) to prevent raveling.

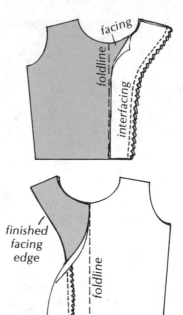

3. Pink the seam allowance to reduce bulk. Bring wrong sides together. Trim any interfacing that extends beyond the fold line (or raw edge in separate facing). If using a fusible, fuse interfacing to facing.

4. Fold faced facing into place (or sew separate facing to garment).

Cut On Self-Interfaced Facing

Eliminate the need for a separate interfacing and finish the facing edge at the same time. Palmer/Pletsch associate, Marta Alto, developed this technique after seeing it on a Calvin Klein shirt.

This technique works only on straight edges like shirt front and back closures and does require more garment fabric. It is best for sheer to lightweight silkies and solid colors (prints may show through). TEST to see if the triple layer of self fabric will be firm enough for a buttonhole.

1. Trim off the extended facing (if any) to the fold line.

2. When cutting out the garment add 2½" from the front edge of fold line. Fold 1¼" once, then 1¼" again to wrong side. Press.

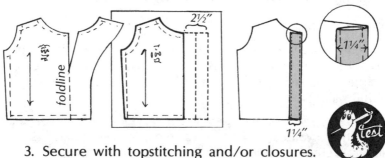

3. Secure with topstitching and/or closures.

Self-Interfaced Shirt Fronts

Self-fabric interfacing can be used for straight sewn-on front shirt bands. Generally the sewn-on band is on the right front side of women's shirts. Caution: prints may shadow through. Cut-on facings won't work because the band folds to the right side — then it would be wrong side out!

1. Cut band twice the desired finished width (usually 2 × 1¼") plus one seam allowance.

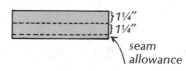

1¼"
1¼"

seam allowance

2. Sew the band right side to the garment wrong side.

3. Turn to right side, fold under one width. Press. Topstitch.

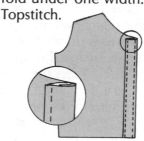

wrong side

wrong side

Hassle-Free Hidden Button Placket

You can totally hide less than desirable buttonholes and buttons that don't quite match! Some patterns include this placket feature, but is is easy to convert most blouse and dress styles. Use this placket on any straight edge closure like a blouse or dress front or back. The neckline edge should be finished with a stand, binding or collar, not a facing.

3½

1" 1" 1" ½"

foldline

A   B C

1. Extend the garment right front piece edge 3½" from the seamline or foldline. This width can be varied with the button size, but a 3½" extension will make a 1" finished placket, a good width for most blouses and dresses with ¼-½" buttons. Mark intervals as shown.

2. Fold and press along the ½" line, the first 1" line and the foldline.

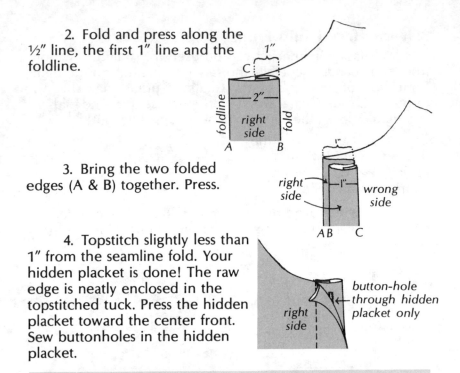

3. Bring the two folded edges (A & B) together. Press.

4. Topstitch slightly less than 1" from the seamline fold. Your hidden placket is done! The raw edge is neatly enclosed in the topstitched tuck. Press the hidden placket toward the center front. Sew buttonholes in the hidden placket.

NOTE: Sew-through buttons are best for this style because the placket should lie flat!

Narrow Uninterfaced Facings

Perfect for tightly woven or knit lightweight silks and silkies as they will show less. Pink the facing to 1¼" total width. Sew the ⅝" seam, grade, understitch and press lightly to the wrong side. Topstitch ⅜" from the finished edge. Finished facing will be ⅝" wide.

NOTE: On very ravel-prone fabrics, I use bias strips for facings instead (see pg. 80) because bias doesn't ravel!

Turned and Stitched Facing

Nice for soft knits like boucle jerseys and interlocks. Not for severe curves or corners. The seam or hem allowance shouldn't be more than ½" to the wrong side. Stitch ⅛" and ⅜" from the fold. DO NOT STRETCH OUT THE EDGE WHILE PRESSING OR STITCHING.

The Swiss Edge

Looks like a napkin edge finish. Use it for firm, woven fabrics or stable knits.
(See pg. 124-125 for instructions.)

The Invisible Facing

When facing a sheer or semi-sheer print, cut facings from a solid color sheer fabric. Organza works well.

CHAPTER EIGHTEEN

Sleeves

Make Sleeves Simple!

Make silky sleeves really easy by selecting easy sleeve styles . . . since silks and silkies drape so beautifully, full, all-in-one and dropped shoulder sleeves are sensational and simple-to-sew.

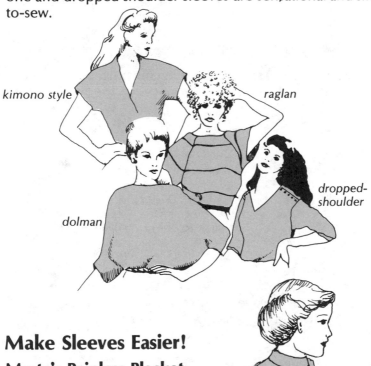

kimono style

raglan

dolman

dropped-shoulder

Make Sleeves Easier!

Marta's Painless Placket

Marta Alto, Palmer/Pletsch Associate and resident speed sewing person, discovered this "in the seam" instant placket a few years ago . . . and made sewing dresses and blouses so much easier for us all.

She recommends painless plackets for straight sleeves, but I've used it on fuller sleeves. Avoid shirt-type sleeves with flatter caps for this technique.

straight sleeve   *full sleeve*

1. Draw a line through the center of the pattern placket markings, parallel to the grain line. Cut along that line.

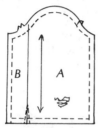 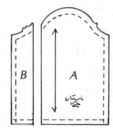

2. Reposition B so that existing stitching lines overlap. Tape together. Add ⅝" seam allowances to the new outside edges.

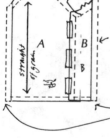 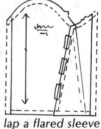

add new seam allowances

these edges should be parallel to the grainline for the underarm curve to be accurate

lap a flared sleeve to keep outer edges parallel

3. Cut sleeves — if the sleeve is straight, cut edge A on the selvage — then further finishing will be unnecessary.

To make a fuller, flared sleeve (more gathered into the cuff) angle seams out equally from both sides.

The more angled the seam, the more bias and stretchy it will be. Make sure the sleeve is long enough by adding at least 1" to the sleeve length. This prevents stretching along the seam.

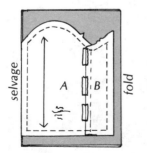 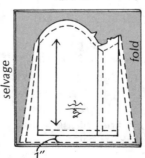

4. Attach the cuffs while sleeve is flat! Trim undercuff ⅛″ smaller on both sides, tapering to nothing at the fold line.

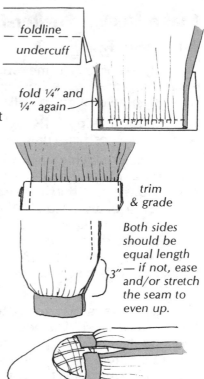

foldline

undercuff

fold ¼″ and ¼″ again

5. Sew the cuff ends right sides together. Trim and grade seams. Turn right sides out. The under cuff is smaller so it will pull to the inside when finished.

trim & grade

6. Begin sewing the sleeve seam 3″ from the bottom of the sleeve.

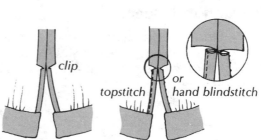

Both sides should be equal length — if not, ease and/or stretch the seam to even up.

3″

7. Press the seam open (over a seam roll). Topstitch ⅜″ from the placket opening edges to finish. Or clip into seam allowances ½″ and turn under the raw edges twice. Finish with topstitching or a hand blindstitch.

clip

topstitch

or hand blindstitch

8. To stitch undercuff to sleeve, "stitch in the ditch" from the right side or tuck seam allowance under and slip-stitch by hand.

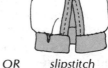

stitch in the ditch   OR   *slipstitch*

Make Sleeves Pucker-Free

Automatic Easing

My publishers came upon this neat technique when researching their book **Sewing Skinner® Ultrasuede® Fabric.** Here is an adaptation for silks and silkies.

1. Cut a strip of 1¼" wide by 13" long Seams Great™, Seam Saver™ or bias-cut sheer to lightweight fabric.

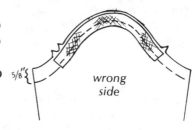

2. Begin stitching bias to the wrong side of the sleeve cap seam allowance at notch. Sew to the sleeve cap just inside of the ⅝" seam line, stretching the strip while sewing from notch to notch. I use a long stitch (8-10/inch) in case adjustment is necessary.

3. Sleeve is now ready to set into armhole. No easing threads to fuss with! If sleeve is still too large, simply pin in ease and stitch. It will automatically ease! If too small, rip out a few intermittent stitches and stretch the bias slightly or start over again stretching the bias strip less when applying.

4. Bias strip remains in sleeve cap seam.

Conventional Sleeve Easing

• Before deciding between the ¾" and ½", or ⅜" and ⅝" basting lines on sleeves, test first. On some silks and silkies, the basting beyond the seam line (¾") can leave needle marks when removed.

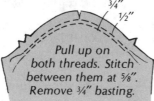

Pull up on both threads. Stitch between them at ⅝". Remove ¾" basting.

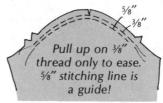

Pull up on ⅜" thread only to ease. ⅝" stitching line is a guide!

• Most, but not all of the ease should be on the sides of the sleeve cap, beginning 1" away from each side of the center snip mark. The fabric is more bias here and much easier to ease.

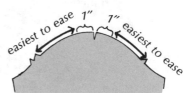

easiest to ease 1"   1" easiest to ease

• When baste stitching, shorten machine stitches to 8/inch and use "ease-plus" — evenly "force feed" the fabric between the feed dog and the foot as you sew. Holding one hand behind the presser foot as shown helps ease-plus.

Stitch Sleeve Into Armhole

1. Use lots of pins to position the sleeve.

2. Machine baste sleeve in (always with sleeve on top). Do not stitch over pins.

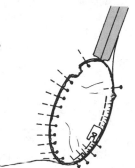

3. Try on. If sleeve is puckered, clip stitching, smooth with fingers and restitch. If it still puckers you may have to make the sleeve cap smaller. Rip sleeve basting from notch to notch over sleeve cap. Slip top of sleeve cap into armhole ⅛-¼", tapering to nothing at the notches. Pin and rebaste.

4. Final stitch over basting and again ¼" away. Trim to ¼" stitching.

NOTE: *Do not clip armhole seam.* Clipping is only for curves that need to be straightened out.

5. Press cap seam allowance only (as shown).

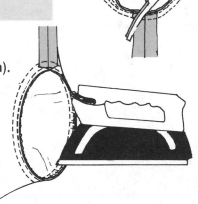

Make Shoulders Shapely

I've noticed that better silk and silky blouses are frequently equipped with soft shoulder shaping. It's easy to make your own self-fabric covered shoulder pads.

Simply buy readymade pads and cover them with fabric. Small readymade pads are available — your pattern will indicate the thickness necessary. If you can't find the right size, cover layers of polyester fleece, like Stacy's ThermoLam® Plus or Bias Polyester Fleece Pellon® with your fabric.

purchased
shoulder pad
or layers
of polyester
fleece

bias line of
fabric

right side of
fabric —
shoulder pad
inside

Try on the garment with shoulder pads pinned in place . . . the edge of the pad should extend ⅜" into the sleeve. Hand stitch to seam allowances.

⅜"

Make Sleeves Fun!

Ruffled Sleeves
(see Chapter 13, pgs 77 & 78)

• Use ruffles as "sleeves" in sleeveless dresses . . . stagger the layers.

• Sew layers of ruffles on a sleeve (while it is still flat, before seaming!)

- Add a ruffle insert:

1. Fold the sleeve pattern in half lengthwise at shoulder top dot and crease. Cut along the crease line. Add ⅝" seam allowance to each cut edge. Cut out sleeves.

add ⅝"
seam
allowance

2. Cut a 3¼" wide ruffle section twice as long as the sleeve center seam (up to three times as long for soft sheers). For a very soft ruffle, cut the ruffle strip on the bias (See pgs. 79 & 80.).

3. Fold the ruffle section in half, right sides together, press.

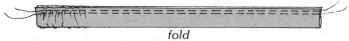

fold

4. Gather the ruffle strip and sew to one side of the sleeve along the center seam.

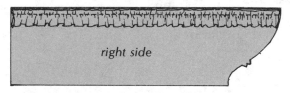

right side

5. Sew the two sleeve halves together. Lightly press the ruffle toward the back of the sleeve. Set sleeve into armhole.

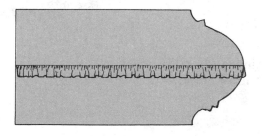

Double Sleeves

For a very short sleeve with no hem, create a "double" sleeve.

1. Cut sleeve piece as shown.

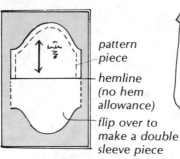

pattern piece

hemline (no hem allowance)

flip over to make a double sleeve piece

2. Sew underarm seam. Press open. Fold sleeves wrong sides together.

3. Set in as usual.

OR, line sleeves with the same or lighter weight fabric in a contrasting color. Simply cut out two sleeves for each one allowing a ⅝" seam along the hemlines.

Sew the sleeves right sides together along the hemline. Press the seam open.

sleeve

lining

Complete as above.

Turn sleeve up, cuff style, to reveal contrast color.

CHAPTER NINETEEN

Collars

Choosing the Right Collar

Pick a pattern with the right collar style for your intended look. Use the following guidelines:

The Collar Pattern		The Collar Look

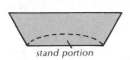
stand portion

Convertible Collar
The straighter the collar the more it will stand up. This type stands at the back of neck, but opens flat in front.

no stand

Peter Pan or Middy Collars
The more curve, the flatter the collar will be.

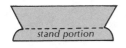
stand portion

Easy Shirt Collar
This has a stand cut on to the collar. The built-in stand gives room for wearing a scarf or tie at neck.

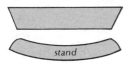
stand

Traditional Shirt Collar
Curve in separate stand allows for closer fit around neck.

stand only

Stand or Band Without a Collar
Who says you have to use the collar?!

Collars are seen so frequently on ready-to-wear blouses but many of the seamsters I know are frustrated with their at-home attempts. It is possible to get a smooth, professional look with lightweight silks and silkies.

Silky Collar Tips

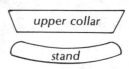

• **Interface the collar.** Test fusibles first on your fabric before fusing them to an upper collar or the stand side that shows. I've had good luck using Easy Knit on the upper collar and stand. It acts as a buffer to the collar seams, making the top layer smooth. If fusing is not satisfactory on the upper collar, use a stitchable (see Chapter 5, pg. 33).

Interface these pieces. (For a firm stand interface its facing, too.)

• **To make a really firm stand,** you can fuse to both the stand and its facing.

• **On lighter weight silks** and silkies the fusible interfacing seam allowances don't need to be trimmed before fusing but on heavier weight fabrics, trim ½" off all interfacing edges.

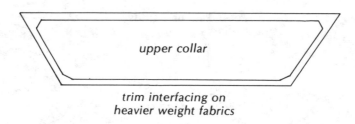

trim interfacing on heavier weight fabrics

• **To make smooth even points** on heavier silkies, trim the interfacing diagonally ¼" into the collar corner before fusing or stitching.

• **Trim the under collar and stand facing** ⅛" as shown to allow for "turn of cloth" so seams won't peek to the right side. Some patterns — blazers for example — provide separate pattern pieces that are already smaller for the under layers.

undercollar   *stand facing*

- **Reinforce corners** by shortening the stitch length as you stitch around points or curves. This minimizes raveling and moves your machine into a slower speed for more accurate stitching.

- **Stitch across the point** one or more diagonal stitches eliminating "dimples."

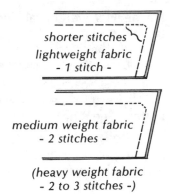

shorter stitches
lightweight fabric
- 1 stitch -

medium weight fabric
- 2 stitches -

(heavy weight fabric
- 2 to 3 stitches -)

- **Stitch directionally.** Have you ever noticed that your collars looked different from side to side? Mine did too until I started stitching from the center to the collar points. (If you start at one side of the collar or stand and stitch to the other, it "grows" as you stitch, making the last section to be stitched a different shape than the first. Stitching them both in the same direction eliminates the problem.) Also use this tip when sewing the stand to the neck edge.

- **Do you ever get a "dimple"** where the stand adjoins the facing edge? Simply cheat a little and sew the band 1/16" over the edge.

dimple here?

←1/16"

- **Eliminate bulk** — trim and grade the seam(s) close to the stitching at the points. Most curves in lightweight silks and silkies can be graded and notched simultaneously by pinking the seam (use small stitches around curves to be pinked).

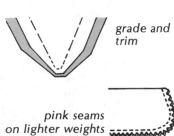

grade and trim

pink seams on lighter weights

For heavier weight fabrics, layer the seam and stagger the notches for durability and smoothness on the right side.

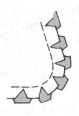

layer and stagger notches

Press seams open over a point presser so edges will turn better. (See Chpt. 12, pg. 69).

Roll collar and facing seams to the underside when pressing so they don't show. If the collar point needs coaxing use a point turner — easy does it!! No scissor points, please!

Fun Collar Ideas

Topstitch lightweight ribbon (satin is good) to top collar before sewing the two layers together.

Bind collars with bias (see Chapter 15) or insert piping (Chapter 16).

Double collars (sometimes included in the pattern). Cut single or double layer and finish with Swiss Edge (see pg. 124-125) or face each layer but do not interface. The top collar is cut slightly smaller along the outer edges so the collar underneath will show.

Use a contrasting color for the stand facing.

Tie front blouses can be beautifully easy! No buttons — but a slit neckline opening that pulls over and ties. The collar/tie is not interfaced.

"Plaited" collar — trim done with a ruffler attachment.

110

CHAPTER TWENTY

Zippers

Zipper Tips

• One inch seam allowances on a zippered seam are easier to handle and more durable than narrower seams.

• Finish seams before inserting the zipper (see pg. 59).

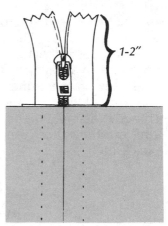

• Use only lightweight synthetic coil zippers.

• Buy zippers 1-2" too long. Extend the zipper top beyond the garment — the slider will then be out of the way for even stitching. Zippers today are self-locking so they don't need to be zipped up to the top to stay up!

• Always machine topstitch zippers in from the side that shows — it's just too hard to "guestimate" if you're sewing straight when stitching from the wrong side.

• Use ½" wide Scotch Brand Magic Transparent Tape as a topstitching guide on all but napped fabrics. Try angling the stitching at the bottom of the zipper placket for a softer line.

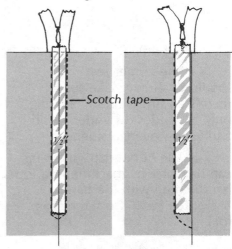

—Scotch tape—

Beautiful Handworked Zippers — Perfect for Silks and Silkies

• Pulling and puckering can be a problem when machine stitching zippers in place on lightweight silks and silkies. That's why I prefer hand stitched zippers in these fabrics.

Hand baste the seam closed and the zipper in. Single strands of silk or lingerie thread mark the least. Machine basting the seam together first can leave holes and puckering when the seam is pulled out.

Using a tiny hand backstitch, a size 10 needle (finer needles allow a finer stitch) and a double strand of the silk or lingerie threads (others will work but the finer types make neater stitches), sew in the zipper. The basting thread will be your stitching guideline. Pull out the basting carefully after completing the backstitch.

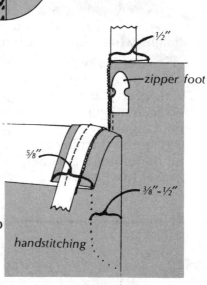

1/4"-3/8"

1/2"

zipper foot

Lapped Zippers

• The zipper teeth shouldn't show. Make sure there's an underlap by pressing only 1/2" under on underlap side and 5/8" on overlap side.

5/8"

3/8"-1/2"

• The "underlap" stitching can be done by machine, the top lap stitching with the hand backstitch 3/8"-1/2" from the seam fold.

handstitching

112

Variation:

For a "no-stitching" underlap; place the zipper wrong side up with teeth next to stitching line. Machine stitch close to the teeth. Then fold to the inside.

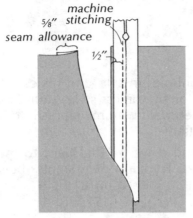

machine
⅝" stitching
seam allowance
½"

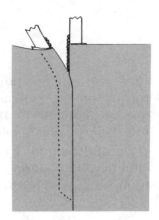

Centered Zippers

• Centered zippers can be taped in place rather than basted. Use Scotch Brand Magic Transparent Tape or basting tape. For this technique, the zipper seam opening should be basted closed by hand before taping. Center zipper over seam and tape in place.

• Hand stitch in the directions shown to minimize distortion, pulling, and puckering.

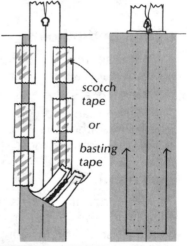

scotch tape

or

basting tape

NOTE: To reinforce lapped or centered hand-worked zippers, especially in tight-fitting styles, machine stitch through each seam allowance and the zipper tape on both sides as shown after handstitching.

hand-stitching

machine stitching

seam allowance

machine stitching

CHAPTER TWENTY-ONE

Beautiful Buttonholes

Yes, you can sew buttonholes in silks and silkies. I too was forever on the lookout for buttonless styles until finally taking a few moments to experiment with my fabric, interfacing and machine stitch variations.

Low and behold, I found it wasn't that hard to make beautiful machine buttonholes. Try a few test samples before "buttonholing" your garment . . . it's a must.

Testing Buttonholes

Try all the buttonhole variables — stitch length and width, tension alternatives, interfacing — before deciding that your sewn wardrobe will remain buttonless.

Since many non-woven interfacings have stability in the lengthwise rather than crosswise direction, make buttonholes in the direction of most stability if stretching is a problem.

Placement Tips

• Horizontal buttonholes should begin ⅛" toward the edge from the center front. Use horizontal buttonholes at points of strain or in closely fitted garments.

• Vertical buttonholes should be positioned on the center front line. Sew buttons on the center front line. Use vertical buttonholes in narrow bands or plackets that limit the buttonhole width, or in fabrics with lots of crosswise stretch, like knits.

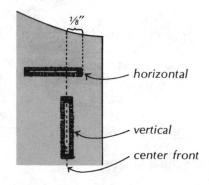

• Do you suffer from blouse bustline gaposis? I did for years. Susan Pletsch clued me in on the cure. Try on the garment — the first button marking should always be at the bust level. Mark all other buttonholes from that point. I usually space them 2-3″ apart. It's impossible for pattern companies to mark this position accurately for you because of varied figure types.

• Buttonholes are on the right-hand side in most women's garments. If you sew the buttonholes in the left side, don't throw away the garment — no one will know but you. Just say you copied expensive European ready-to-wear — it's all buttoned unisex!

• Be creative in your buttonhole placement. "Group" buttonholes as shown.

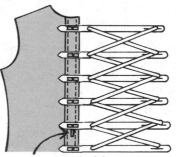

How to Mark Buttonholes — Lots of Options

• By far the simplest way to space buttonholes is to use a marker like the Simflex. It folds up and extends accordian-style. The "windows" at the end of the spokes will allow you to mark the horizontal button-holes and the top ends of vertical buttonholes.

marking vertical buttonholes

• If you don't have a Simflex marker, use a ruler (see-through types are nice).

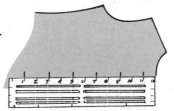

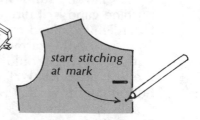

- If you have a buttonhole foot that measures the stitching length as you sew, or a built-in buttonholer with preset buttonhole length, just mark the point to begin stitching.

start stitching at mark

- Keep a small sewing gauge in hand to double-check the buttonhole length and position while sewing.

- Use your machine buttonhole foot for easy placement. Align the back of the foot with the seam edge for each buttonhole. Stitch in the same direction for each buttonhole.

What to Mark With

- Mark with a washable marking pen, like Dritz Mark-B-Gone™ or Traum's Wonder Marker™. Some of the newer types even disappear within 48 hours without sponging away — better work fast. Test on your fabric first to make sure the marks do come out.

- Scotch Brand Magic Transparent Tape — mark the buttonhole length on the tape with pencil before taping to the garment.

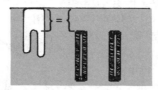

- Hand baste a single strand of silk thread horizontally and vertically to mark the buttonhole without leaving marks on the fabric. Stitch next to the thread, not over it so it will be easy to remove the basting after stitching.

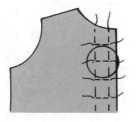

How to Get Smooth Pucker-free Buttonholes

1. Pin or baste a strip of "Stitch-n-Tear" Pellon or "Stitch and Tear" by Handler Textiles to the right side of your garment over the button-hole area. This will provide pucker prevention at button-hole ends.

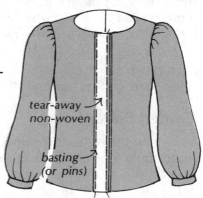

tear-away non-woven

basting (or pins)

2. Mark the button-holes with washable marker on the tear-away non-woven.

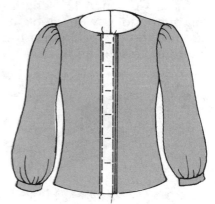

3. Stitch the button-holes through the nonwoven and all fabric layers.

4. Tear away the tear-away interfacing.

Buttonhole Tips

• Use good quality thread that is the right size. I like finer threads for lightweight fabrics — lingerie and silk both work well. It's easier to obtain even tension by using the same thread in the top and bobbin.

• Start with a new needle. Have you ever noticed how many buttonholes in silk and silky garments have snag lines extending from the buttonhole stitching? You can prevent it with a new needle that is the right size.

• Adjust the machine tension to make a "pretty" zigzag stitch on top. I usually loosen the upper tension slightly to get more thread coverage on the right side. Experiment with different stitch lengths and widths.

• Try a variation of "taut sewing" (see pg. 54) when stitching. Hold the fabric taut between your forefingers on either side of the buttonhole while stitching.

Corded Buttonholes

1. If the buttonhole needs stabilizing, try cording. If your buttonhole foot doesn't have a hook on the back for cording, insert a pin in the right side of the fabric aligning it with the center line of the buttonhole.

2. Cut an 8-12″ length of buttonhole twist. Hook it around the pin or around the buttonhole foot hook.

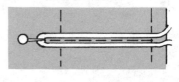

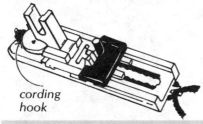

cording hook

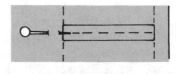

NOTE: For a lighter buttonhole, a few strands of regular sewing thread twisted together can be used instead of buttonhole twist. Many sewing machine manuals show how to twist thread together using the bobbin winder.

3. Hold the cord or thread(s) taut while stitching the buttonhole. Stitch over, but not through the cord. Finish the buttonhole.

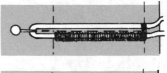

4. Draw up the cord slightly, pulling the ends until the loop disappears under the stitching. Thread a needle with the cord ends and bring to the back, tie and anchor in the machine stitching.

draw up cord

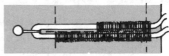

Cutting the Buttonhole

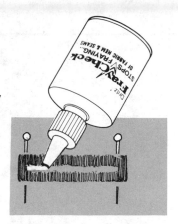

1. Carefully run a line of Fray Check® between the buttonhole stitching lines. Allow to dry.

2. Place pins through the ends of the buttonholes. These pins will prevent cutting through the stitching when cutting the buttonhole open.

3. To cut the buttonhole: My artist/partner cuts my buttonholes with an X-acto® knife! Now not all of us are blessed with such talented help but we can learn from her effortless precision. Use a clean X-acto knife or Olfa's Technic Knife and cut down the center of each buttonhole, pin to pin. Sharp seam rippers can also be used, but be careful!

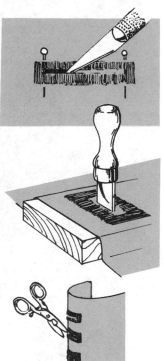

4. Or, try this new notion for buttonhole cutting. Look for a "buttonhole cutter" — a straight edge cutter and wooden cutting block.

If you're using scissors, sharp embroidery or special buttonhole scissors work best. Clip open by folding the buttonhole in half.

5. Don't fret if you cut a few threads. Either touch up with Fray Check® and leave as is, OR restitch the clipped section.

NOTE: On some medium to heavier weight fabrics I restitch the entire buttonhole after it's clipped (usually too much thread and bulk for lighter weight silks and silkies). This gives additional thread coverage for a ravel-free buttonhole.

CHAPTER TWENTY-TWO
Hems are Everywhere

Hems in silks and silky-types aren't difficult, just different. Use the techniques described in this chapter for much more than bottom edge hems but for collar, cuff, ruffle and scarf edges. Stay elegantly simple and use just one decorative hem technique per garment.

Tips for Hems

• Plan a no-hem for ruffles. Align the hemline along the selvage.

• Less is best on silkies. Tapes, laces and on some, even a line of machine stitching will show through or press through to the right side. Pinking is enough for most lightweight silks and silkies.

• Avoid hemming with a fusible web. It's too stiff for these silks and silkies.

• Minimize bulk before turning up the hem by trimming seams in hem allowance.

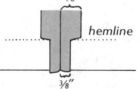

• Lightning won't strike if you leave tuck-in blouses unhemmed. Pati Palmer just pinks the lower edges of shirts (says she doesn't need any "extra bulk" through the hipline).

• Try hemming the edge first, then seaming, especially when sewing a machine rolled hem with the attachment. To prevent the seam end from showing on the hem edge, fold the seam allowance edges up to the seam stitching line and carefully machine stitch in place.

←hemmed edges→

fold up seam edges and
stitch in place

Deciding Hem Depth and Technique

Garment Silhouette & Hem Depth	Machine (M) or Hand Sewn (H)	Best Hem Techniques	Type of Fabric Swatch for Testing Technique
Straight (⅛"-3")	M M M H	Machine Rolled (with attachment) Swiss Edge Hem Scarf Edge Hem Perfectly Invisible Hand Hem	Straight hem test swatch (crosswise or lengthwise grain)
A-line (⅛"-3")	M M H	Machine Rolled (without attachment) Topstitched Hem Perfectly Invisible Hem	Curved hem test swatch
Flared/ Circular (⅛"-¼")	M M M M H	Machine Rolled (without attachment) Scarf Edge Hem Topstitched Hem Swiss Edge Hem Easy Hand Rolled Hem	Very curved hem test swatch
Bias (⅛"-¼")	M M M M H	Machine Rolled (without attachment) Swiss Edge Hem Lettuce Leaf Hem Topstitched Hem Easy Hand Rolled Hem	Bias hem test swatch

Machine Hems

NOTE: To prevent jamming at the beginning of a hem pull a long tail of top and bottom thread. Hold onto the thread as you begin stitching so thread and fabric won't jam down into the hole.

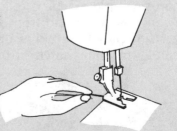

Machine Rolled Hem (without attachment)

Uses: any straight, curved or bias edge.

1. Trim the hem allowance to ½".

2. Turn up the hem ¼" and stitch in place close to the fold.

3. Turn up the hem again ¼". Stitch in place approximately ⅛" from the folded edge.

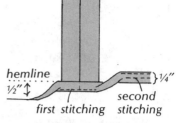

hemline

½" ↕

first stitching

second stitching

}¼"

Variation: The second row of stitching can be a zig-zag or blind hemstitch for a decorative finish. Experiment with different width and length zig-zag stitching.

Machine Rolled Hem (with attachment)

Uses: any straight edge. Curved edges are very difficult to hold in the hemmer.

> NOTE: To learn machine-rolled hemming, use a fabric that's not too slippery, like cotton broadcloth. Then graduate to the more slippery types.

I've found silks and rayons easier to hem with the attachment than other silkies. If the fabric's too heavy, however, it will not fit into the attachment.

1. Read your machine manual and find your rolled hem foot. Techniques will vary from machine to machine. Most machine manufacturers offer several different rolled hem foot widths. The medium to wide ones are the easiest to use.

2. Always, always test this technique first on a sample garment swatch. The results can be beautiful, but it takes practice even for experienced seamsters.

3. Trim the hem allowances to ¼"-½". This will vary with hemmer width, so test.

4. Machine baste tear-away non-woven interfacing to the seam side of the hem edge.

5. Fold up ¼" or so to the wrong side of the garment and slip the tear-away interfacing into the hemmer.

6. Start stitching, controlling the "fabric feed" with one hand and holding up the fabric feeding in as shown. The degree the fabric is held up will vary the roll width. The higher it is held up, the more the fabric will roll. Try to hold the fabric at the same angle in front of the foot for the entire hem length. Roll under the edge while feeding it into the foot. It may help to hold the hem slightly to the left in front of the foot.

tear-away

side seam edge

¼"

7. Sew the garment seam(s).

NOTE: To fix a hem if your hemmer runs off the hem edge: After you've run off, start the roll again 2" or so from the run-off point. Finish the hem, change to a regular sewing foot and topstitch the "unhemmed" section in place joining stitching lines. Pull threads to wrong side and tie.

turn under and topstitch

Mock French Seam

Once you've mastered the machine rolled hem, you can use the foot for a very narrow, straight "Mock French Seam."

The Swiss Edge Hem

Uses: Any straight, curved or bias edge. This hem is not recommended for very loosely woven fabrics. To facilitate continuous sewing you can "round-off" corners.

1. Set your machine on a medium width zigzag, about 12-15 stitches per inch.

2. Trim hem allowances to ½".

3. On the hemline stitch directly over a few strands of regular sewing thread, or one strand of buttonhole twist or pearl cotton.

cord

NOTE: The heavier the cording thread the more obvious the hem will be and the closer the zigzagging will need to be to cover it. A cording foot, available with many late model machines, may make this step easier although it is not mandatory.

4. With very sharp scissors, trim to the zigzagging.

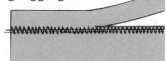

5. Zigzag again with the same or slightly wider stitch over the cut edge.

The Scarf Edge Variation

Uses: This hem finish isn't just for scarves . . . it's a nice lightweight hem for any straight, curved or bias edge. If stretching and curling are problems, the stitching should be done with the ease-plus technique (see pg. 103).

1. Trim the hem allowance to ½-1".

2. Straight stitch along the hemline.

3. Fold the hem allowance to the wrong side right on the stitching line.

4. Zig-zag with a close, medium width stitch along the edge, enclosing the fold.

5. Trim the hem allowance to the stitching.

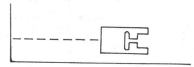

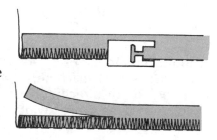

The Hand Hems
Perfectly Invisible Hem

Uses: A wide hem for straight, only slightly curved (easing edgestitching will show through to the right side on most silkies) and bias edges.

1. Trim the hem allowance to no wider than 3".

2. Finish the hem edge on woven fabrics with pinking shears. Knits will need no hem finish at all. Straight edge stitching (¼" from edge) is optional but often shows through to the right side.

3. Lightly steam the hem in place. Don't press along the hem edge — this will leave an impression on the right side.

4. Turn back the pinked edge ¼" or so with your finger. With a running stitch and a single thread strand, catch only a thread or two of the garment, then catch the hem. Small hand stitching needles help (size 10).

The stitches should not lie on top of each other — this causes too much pull and unsightly marks on the right side. Instead, form a "zigzag" hand stitching pattern. Pull and loosen the stitches every 6" or so and knot the thread in the hem allowance to secure.

An Easy Hand-Rolled Hem

Uses: A narrow hem for straight, curved (more difficult) or bias edges. Super for soft scarf edges.

NOTE: Use the finest needle (size 10) and thread (lingerie or silk types are good). also need bright light for accuracy. Also the roll width can be varied although narrower hems can be more difficult to sew.

1. Trim hem allowance to ½".

2. Turn up ¼" to the wrong side and machine stitch in place. Do not press.

3. Turn up another ¼" and blindstitch in place. Stitches should be about ¼"-⅜" apart. The first row of machine stitching should fall directly on the fold, serving as a hem width guideline.

INDEX

More Products from Palmer/Pletsch!

Palmer/Pletsch publishes a whole series of easy to use, information-filled sewing how-to books. Look for their books and new video in local fabric stores or order through Palmer/Pletsch by copying the form below.

new!

Original ROO
A children's story that makes sewing fun!

Qty.	Description	Price	Total	Qty.	Description	Price	Total
	New Creative Serging	$6.95			Sensational Silk	$6.95	
	Sewing With Sergers	6.95			Mother Pletsch's Painless Sewing *Revised*	6.95	
	Clothes Sense	6.95			Sew Big...a fashion guide for the fuller figure	6.95	
	Pants for Any Body *Revised*	6.95			Sew a Beautiful Wedding	6.95	
	Easy, Easier, Easiest Tailoring *Revised*	6.95			Original Roo (Children's Story)	5.95	
	Sewing Skinner® Ultrasuede® Fabric	4.95			NEW VIDEO—Sewing Today The Time Saving Way	29.95	

Col. 1 total

Name _____

Address _____

City/State _____ Zip_____

☐ Visa   ☐ MasterCard   ☐ Check Enclosed

_____

Exp. Date_____

If Ordering Video:

☐ VHS

☐ Beta

Col. 1 total

Col. 2 total

For spiral bindings, add $2.00 per book

Shipping/handling   1.50

TOTAL

Please allow 4-6 weeks for delivery